Harvard University

Syllabus for an Elementary Course in Constitutional Government

Together with the Articles of Confederation, and Constitution of the United States

Harvard University

Syllabus for an Elementary Course in Constitutional Government
Together with the Articles of Confederation, and Constitution of the United States

ISBN/EAN: 9783337191245

Printed in Europe, USA, Canada, Australia, Japan

Cover: Foto ©Suzi / pixelio.de

More available books at **www.hansebooks.com**

Syllabus

FOR AN ELEMENTARY COURSE

IN

Constitutional Government,

TOGETHER WITH THE

ARTICLES OF CONFEDERATION, AND CONSTITUTION OF THE UNITED STATES.

ALSO, SELECTED PASSAGES RELATING TO SOME PORTIONS OF THE COURSE.

———

[HISTORY 2 IN HARVARD COLLEGE.]

———

CAMBRIDGE, MASS.:

W. H. WHEELER, PUBLISHER AND PRINTER.

1884.

ELEMENTARY BOOKS.

Each member of the class is expected to use either Amos's "Primer of the English Constitution" or Fonblanque's "How We are Governed." The following works will be found useful for reading and reference :—

FOR ENGLAND : "Central Government," by H. D. Trail [Citizen Series]; The "House of Commons," by R. Palgrave,—a description of the life of the House; "Handbook of Parliamentary Procedure," by H. W. Lucy; The "Electorate and the Legislature," by Spencer Walpole [Citizen Series]; Chap. III of Freeman's Growth of the English Constitution, also his essay on Presidential Government [Historical Essays Vol. I], and his article on the Power of Dissolution [N.A. Rev., Aug. '79]; Gladstone's "Kin Beyond Sea"; Bagehot's "English Constitution,"—very instructive though wrong on some American matters. The "Crown and its Advisers," by A. C. Ewald,—useful as a simple statement of the Tory view of the Constitution. Whitaker's Almanac is useful for lists of public offices, salaries, members of Parliament, the Privy Council, etc., etc. D. B. Eaton's Civil Service in Great Britain; A. C. Ewald's "Guide to the Home Civil Service." Larger works : Cox's "Institutions of the English Goverment"; Todd's "Parliamentary Government"; J. S. Mill's "Representative Government"; "Wolsey's Political Science"; "The Cabinet Lawyer"; Escott's "England."

FOR THE UNITED STATES : Bancroft's "History of the Formation of the Constitution," Vol. 2 ; McMaster's "History of the People of the United States," Vol. 1 ; Hildreth's "History of the United States," Chap. XLVII Elliot's "Debates," Vol. I and V ; Cooley's "Constitutional Law."

FOR FRANCE : "L'Organization française," by Alphonse Bertrand [Paris, A. Quantin]; "La France," "Le Department" and "La Commune," by Maurice Block [Paris, Hetzel & Cie.]; "Le Livre du Petit Gitoyen," by Jules Simon [Paris, Hachette & Cie].

FOR GERMANY: "The German Constitution from 1815 to 1871," by A. Nicholson; "Katechismus des Deutschen Reiches," by W. Zeller [Leipsic, J. J. Weber]; "Staatsrecht des Deutschen Reiches," by P. Zorn [Berlin, J. Guttentag]; "Handbuch der Deutschen Verfassungen," by F. Stoerk [Leipsic, Duncker & Humblot]

SYLLABUS.

THE ENGLISH CONSTITUTION.

1. *General Features of the English Government.* A monarchy in which the prerogatives of the Crown have become subject to the control of Parliament. The Constitution a growth, rather than a deliberate creation; for the most part unwritten; influence of custom and of precedent.

2. *Prerogatives of the Crown.* "The Queen can do no wrong." Ministerial responsibility. All acts of government must be done through Ministers. The Queen has the right to be consulted, the right to encourage, and the right to warn. Distinction between prerogative and influence. The Queen in legislation. The Royal Speech and the Address. The Veto power. The Civil List.

3. *The Cabinet.* Its importance. How its members are selected. The offices they hold. The Cabinet has no legal recognition. The Cabinet and the Ministry. The Cabinet and the Privy Council. The Queen in Council. Orders in Council. The Ministry and the Parliament. The resignation of a Ministry.

4. *The Prime Minister.* Nominally chosen by the Queen, but in reality designated by the people. His relations with the other ministers. Effect of his resignation. The Premiership not an office but a position; has no legal recognition. Compare the English Prime Minister with the American President. The Cabinet in each system.

5. *The House of Lords.* Lords Spiritual and Temporal. Representative Peers. Grades of the Peerage. Peers by Writ and Peers by Patent. Abeyance of a Peerage. Peers of the United Kingdom. Irish Peers. Scotch Peers. Law Lords. Lords of Appeal. Peeresses in their own right. Courtesy titles of Peerage. The Speaker of the Lords. The Woolsack. Usher of the Black Rod. The House of Lords since 1832. A "veto of delay." Quorum in the House of Lords.

6. (*a*) *House of Commons.* Number of Members.
Quorum. Counting out. County Members and Borough
Members [Knights and Burgesses]. Representatives of
the Universities. Peers in the House of Commons. The
Speaker not a Party leader. The Mace. The Treas-
ury Bench. The Gangway. The Bar of the House.
The Cross-benches. The Sergeant at Arms.

(*b*) Orders of the Day and Notices of Motion. The
Order Book. Government Days and Private Members'
Days. Committee of Supply. "Grievance before Sup-
ply." The Budget. The Budget Speech. Committee of
Ways and Means. The Deputy Speaker. The Consol-
idated Fund. Consolidated Funds.

(*c*) Stages in the passage of a bill. The Second reading. Committee Stage. Report progress. The three
[six] months' hoist. Freedom of Debate. "Obstruction."
.Naming a member. The Clôture. Urgency. The "previous question" [English and American use]. The new
Standing Committees. Public and Private Bills. A
division of the House. The "Whips."

(*d*) Adjournment; prorogation; dissolution. The Sep-
tennial Act. Writs of Election. The Chiltern Hundreds.'
Reëlection. Nomination Day [old and new]. Contested
and Uncontested Elections. Controverted Elections [Elec-
tion Petitions]. Election Judges. Election Expenses.
Corrupt Practices Acts. Suspension of the Writ. County
Franchise and Borough Franchise. Freeholders. Forty
Shilling Freeholders. Fagot Voters. Leaseholders.
Copyholders. Occupiers. Household Suffrage. Lod-
ger Franchise. The Ballot Act. "Three-Cornered" Constituencies.

7. The principle of unity and coöperation in the English system. How standing disagreements or deadlocks
are prevented. The Ministers as intermediaries between
the two Houses and between the Houses and the Queen.
How the fact that the ministers are also leaders of Parliament gives strength and efficiency both to Parliament and
the Executive. Compare with the plan of separation of
powers and mutual check. How the English system pro-
vides *training* for high office, and avoids unnecessary
changes. Smoothness and certainty of change when
demanded. English Parties: Whig and Tory; Liberal
and Conservative. The Radicals. Irish Home Rulers.

8. The chief Ministerial Offices. Offices permanently in commission [Lord High Treasurer and Lord High Admiral]. First Lord. Junior Lords. Ministers without departmental duties. Permanent Under Secretary. Parliamentary Under Secretary. Joint Secretaries to the Treasury. Lord Lieutenant of Ireland; the Chief Secretary. The Lord Advocate (Scotland). The government of the Indian Empire; Viceroy and Council; Secretary of State and Council. "Responsible Government" in the Colonies.

9. Downing Street. Whitehall. St Stephen's. Court of St. James. The Horse Guards. Patronage; Limited Competition; Open Competition; Superannuation.

10. *The Judicial System.* (*a*) Common Law and Equity. Quarter Sessions. County Courts. The Old Courts of Common Law [Queen's Bench; Common Pleas; Exchequer: Exchequer Chamber]. The Twelve [fifteen] Judges; Justices and Barons. Westminster Hall. Circuits; Assizes; *Nisi Prius*; Verdict; Judgment. Presentment; Indictment. The Court in *banc.* The Court of Chancery; Lord High Chancellor; Master of the Rolls. Injunction. Subpoena. Remedial Jurisdiction. House of Lords; Law Lords.

(*b*) Consistory Courts; Court of Arches. Writs of Prohibition. Admiralty Court. Judicial Committee of the Privy Council.

(*c*) Inns of Court. Barrister; Attorney; Solicitor. Proctor. Attorney General. Solicitor General. Queen's Counsel.

(*d*) The recent reforms of the Judicial System. Fusion of Law and Equity. Union of Courts as Divisions of one High Court. The new Queen's Bench division. Her Majesty's Court of [Intermediate] Appeal. House of Lords; Lords of Appeal. The Lords of Appeal to constitute the Judicial Committee of the Privy Council.

UNITED STATES.

1. Representation in the Congress under the Articles of Confederation. Extent and character of the legislative power. Provision for raising a revenue, and attempts made

to reform it. Executive authority under the Articles.
Lack of an administrative system. No judicial system.
State Sovereignty.

2. The Annapolis Convention. The Federal Convention. Virginia Plan and Jersey Plan. General sketch of
the proceedings of the Convention. Questions found most
difficult to settle. Chief points in which the Constitution as finally adopted differed from the original plan
reported from Committee of the Whole. Compromises.

3. Topics and questions relating to the Constitution.*

(*a*) The right to vote in the election of Representatives.
The rule for the apportionment of Representatives before
and since the adoption of the Slavery Amendments. How
are vacancies in the Senate and H. of R. filled? What
authority confers the right to vote in the election of the
President? The purpose and occasion of the XIIth
Amendment. The theoretical advantages of Indirect election. Rise of the National Conventions.

(*b*) Persons liable to Impeachment. Diminished importance of Impeachment in England. Offices to which
Members of Congress can not be appointed. Grounds of
the controversy as to powers of taxation conferred on Congress. Practical working of the clause giving the H. of
R. the sole right to originate revenue bills. Compare
our procedure in financial legislation with the English
method. How may a bill become a law without the President's approval? Explain " Pocket Veto." Declarations
of war and treaties of peace, — how made by the United
States (compare with England, France and Germany).

(*c*) State the provisions of the Constitution relating to
each of the following subjects (also give definitions):
Letters of Marque; attainder; corruption of blood;
treason; *ex post facto* laws; direct taxes; bills of credit;
legal tender; reprieves and pardons; export duties; right
of petition; search warrants; excessive bail; *habeas
corpus.* In what cases and by whom may the privilege of
the writ of Habeas Corpus be suspended?

(*d*) Traces of Slavery in the Constitution. Fugitives
from Labor; the Fugitive Slave Act of 1850. Effect of the
Slavery Amendments on the Apportionment of Represen-

---

* Only the less obvious points are touched upon

tatives. Constitutional position of the Indian tribes living within the territory of the United States.

(*e*) Is the control of the Senate over appointments to be regarded as beneficial? The power of Dismissal. The amended Tenure of Office act. Appointments which do not need the approval of the Senate. Reform of the Civil Service.

(*f*) Provisions of the Constitution in reference to Compensation of Congressmen and salaries of the Judges and the President. Arguments for and against a salaried legislature. Practice of England, France and Germany.

(*g*) Diminished importance of safeguards against executive tyranny in our day. Guarantees for honest and efficient administration more needful. These more difficult to provide. The English system of staking everything on the zeal and intelligence of the House of Commons,—giving it, practically, unlimited powers of inquiry and control. Compare with the method of multifarious popular elections for fixed terms, independent action, and divided responsibility on the part of those elected. Distrust of legislative bodies observable in recent State Constitutions. The adoption of biennial sessions. Restrictions on powers and pay. Effects of the exclusion of office holders from the legislature. Lack of responsible leadership. Seclusion and silence of the Executive.

(*h*) Explain the terms original, appellate, concurrent, and exclusive as applied to jurisdiction. Extent of the original jurisdiction of the Supreme Court. Effect of the XIth Amendment on the judicial power of the United States. Composition and jurisdiction of the Circuit Courts. Concurrent jurisdiction of State and United States' Courts. Transfer of causes, and appeals, from State Courts to the courts of the United States. The right of trial by Jury. Appeals from the Circuit Courts to the Supreme Court. Need of more speedy decision of appeals. Source of the judicial power to declare acts of Congress unconstitutional and void. Have the English courts this power in relation to acts for Parliament?

(*i*) The exact provision for amendment of the Constitution (Distinguish the two modes.) Compare with England, France, and Germany.

FRANCE.

The President: mode of election; term of office; not responsible (except for treason). Choice and appointment of Ministers; their individual and collective responsibility. The Senate: election of Senators; Life Senators (1875-1884). The Chamber of Deputies; *Scrutin d'Arrondissement* and *Scrutin de Liste*. Power of dissolution. National Assembly. Parties in France. Frequency of Ministerial changes. Position and rights of ministers in the Chambers.

Le Bureau. Les Bureaux. La Commission d'Initiatif. Rapporteurs. First and Second *Délibération. Tour d'Inscription. La Tribune. La Clôture. Urgence. Question Préalable. Interpellation. Ordre du jour motivé. La Commission du Budget.*

GERMANY.

Federal character of the Imperial Constitution; its basis of treaties. Preponderance of Prussia. The Emperor. Nature of the *Bundesrath.* Composition of the *Reichstag.* Relations between the two bodies. The Prussian *Landtag.* The Three-class system. Weakness of the representative bodies in Germany.

I.

ARTICLES OF CONFEDERATION

AND PERPETUAL UNION, BETWEEN THE STATES OF NEW HAMPSHIRE, MASSACHUSETTS BAY, RHODE ISLAND AND PROVIDENCE PLANTATIONS, CONNECTICUT, NEW YORK, NEW JERSEY. PENNSYLVANIA, DELAWARE, MARYLAND, VIRGINIA, NORTH CAROLINA, SOUTH CAROLINA, AND GEORGIA.

ARTICLE I.

The style of this confederacy shall be, "THE UNITED STATES OF AMERICA."

ARTICLE II.

Each State retains its sovereignty, freedom, and independence, and every power, jurisdiction and right. which is not. by this Confederation, expressly delegated to the United States in Congress assembled.

ARTICLE III.

The said States hereby severally enter into a firm league of friendship with each other, for their common defence, the security of their liberties, and their mutual and general welfare ; binding themselves to assist each other against all force offered to, or attacks made upon, them, or any of them, on account of religion, sovereignty, trade, or any other pretence whatever.

ARTICLE IV.

The better to secure and perpetuate mutual friendship and intercourse among the people of the different States in this Union, the free inhabitants of each of these States, paupers, vagabonds, and fugitives from justice, excepted, shall be entitled to all privileges and immunities of free citizens in the several States ; and the people of each State shall have free ingress and regress to and from any other State ; and shall enjoy therein all the privileges of trade and commerce, subject to the same duties, impositions, and restrictions, as the inhabitants thereof respectively ; provided, that such restriction shall not extend so far as to prevent the removal of property imported into any State, to any other State of which the owner is an inhabitant; provided also, that no imposition, duties, or restriction, shall be laid by any State, on the property of the United States, or either of them.

If any person guilty of, or charged with, treason, felony, or other high misdemeanor, in any State, shall flee from justice, and be found in any of the United States, he shall, upon demand of the governor or executive power of the State from which he fled, be delivered up, and removed to the State having jurisdiction of his offence.

Full faith and credit shall be given in each of these States to the records, acts and judicial proceedings, of the courts and magistrates of every other State.

ARTICLE V.

For the more convenient management of the general interests of the United States, delegates shall be annually appointed in such manner as the legislature of each State shall direct, to meet in Congress on the first Monday in November, in every year, with a power reserved to each State to recall its delegates, or any of them, at any time within the year, and send others in their stead, for the remainder of the year.

No State shall be represented in Congress by less than two, nor by more than seven, members; and no person shall be capable of being a delegate for more than three years in any term of six years; nor shall any person, being a delegate, be capable of holding any office under the United States, for which he, or another for his benefit, receives any salary, fees, or emolument of any kind.

Each State shall maintain its own delegates in a meeting of the States, and while they act as members of the committee of the States.

In determining questions in the United States in Congress assembled, each State shall have one vote.

Freedom of speech and debate in Congress shall not be impeached or questioned in any court or place out of Congress; and the members of Congress shall be protected in their persons from arrests and imprisonment, during the time of their going to and from, and attendance on, Congress, except for treason, felony, or breach of the peace.

ARTICLE VI.

No State, without the consent of the United States in Congress assembled, shall send any embassy to, or receive any embassy from, or enter into any conference, agreement, alliance, or treaty, with any king, prince, or state ; nor shall any person, holding any office of profit, or trust, under the United States, or any of them, accept of any present, emolument, office, or title, of any kind whatever, from any king, prince, or foreign state ; nor shall the United States in Congress assembled, or any of them, grant any title of nobility.

No two or more States shall enter into any treaty, confederation, or alliance whatever, between them, without the consent of the United States in Congress assembled, specifying accurately the purposes for which the same is to be entered into, and how long it shall continue.

No State shall lay any imposts or duties which may interfere with any stipulations in treaties entered into. by the United States in Congress assembled, with any king, prince, or state, in pursuance of any treaties, already proposed by Congress to the courts of France and Spain.

No vessels of war shall be kept up, in time of peace, by any State, except such number only, as shal be deemed necessary, by the United States in Congress assembled, for the defence of such State, or its trade ; nor shall any body of forces be kept up by any State, in time of peace, except such number only, as in the judgment of the United States in Congress assembled, shall be deemed requisite to garrison the forts necessary for the defence of such State ; but every State shall always keep up a well-regulated and disciplined militia, sufficiently armed and accoutred ; and shall provide and constantly have ready for use, in public stores, a due number of field-pieces and tents, and a proper quantity of arms, ammunition, and camp equipage.

No state shall engage in any war, without the consent of the United States in Congress assembled, unless such State be actually invaded by enemies, or shall have received certain advice of a resolution being formed by some nation of Indians to invade such State, and the danger is so imminent as not to admit of a delay, till the United States in Congress assembled can be consulted ; nor shall any State grant commissions to any ships or vessels of war, nor letters of marque or reprisal, except it be after a declaration of war by the United States in Congress assembled ; and then only against the kingdom or state, and the subjects thereof, against which war has been so declared, and under such regulations as

shall be established by the United States in Congress assembled ;
unless such State be infested by pirates, in which case vessels of war
may be fitted out for that occasion, and kept so long as the danger
shall continue, or until the United States in Congress assembled
shall determine otherwise.

ARTICLE VII.

When land forces are raised by any State for the common defence, all officers of, or under, the rank of colonel, shall be appointed by the legislature of each State, respectively, by whom
such forces shall be raised, or in such manner as such State shall
direct; and all vacancies shall be filled up by the State which first
made the appointment.

ARTICLE VIII.

All charges of war, and all other expenses that shall be incurred
for the common defence, or general welfare, and allowed by the
United States in Congress assembled, shall be defrayed out of a
common treasury, which shall be supplied by the several States in
proportion to the value of all land within each State, granted to,
or surveyed for, any person, as such land and the buildings and
improvements thereon shall be estimated, according to such mode
as the United States in Congress assembled shall, from time to
time, direct and appoint. The taxes for paying that proportion,
shall be laid and levied by the authority and direction of the legislatures of the several States, within the time agreed upon by the
United States in Congress assembled.

ARTICLE IX.

The United States in Congress assembled, shall have the sole
and exclusive right and power of determining on peace and war,
except in the cases mentioned in the sixth article : Of sending
and receiving ambassadors : Entering into treaties and alliances ;
provided that no treaty of commerce shall be made, whereby the
legislative power of the respective States shall be restrained from
imposing such imposts and duties on foreigners as their own people
are subjected to, or from prohibiting the exportation or importation
of any species of goods or commodities whatever : Of establishing
rules for deciding, in all cases, what captures on land or water
shall be legal ; and in what manner prizes, taken by land or naval
forces, in the service of the United States, shall be divided or

appropriated : Of granting letters of marque and reprisal in times of peace : Appointing courts for the trial of piracies and felonies, committed on the high seas ; and establishing courts, for receiving and determining, finally, appeals in all cases of captures ; provided, that no member of Congress shall be appointed a judge of any of the said courts.

The United States in Congress assembled shall also be the last resort, on appeal, in all disputes and differences now subsisting, or that hereafter may arise, between two or more States. concerning boundary, jurisdiction, or any other cause whatever ; which authority shall always be exercised in the manner following : Whenever the legislative or executive authority, or lawful agent, of any State, in controversy with another, shall present a petition to Congress, stating the matter in question, and praying for a hearing, notice thereof shall be given, by order of Congress, to the legislative or executive authority of the other State in controversy ; and a day assigned for the appearance of the parties by their lawful agents, who shall then be directed to appoint, by joint consent, commissioners or judges, to constitute a court for hearing and determining the matter in question : but if they cannot agree. Congress shall name three persons, out of each of the United States ; and from the list of such persons each party shall alternately strike out one, the petitioners beginning, until the number shall be reduced to thirteen ; and from that number, not less than seven, nor more than nine, names, as Congress shall direct, shall, in the presence of Congress, be drawn out, by lot ; and the persons whose names shall be so drawn. or any five of them, shall be commissioners or judges, to hear and finally determine the controversy. so always as a major part of the judges, who shall hear the cause. shall agree in the determination. And if either party shall neglect to attend at the day appointed, without showing reasons which Congress shall judge sufficient, or being present shall refuse to strike, the Congress shall proceed to nominate three persons out of each State ; and the Secretary of Congress shall strike in behalf of such party absent or refusing ; and the judgment and sentence of the court, to be appointed in the manner before prescribed, shall be final and conclusive. And if any of the parties shall refuse to submit to the authority of such court, or to appear, or defend their claim or cause, the court shall, nevertheless, proceed to pronounce sentence or judgment, which shall in like manner be final and decisive ; the judgment, or sentence, and other proceedings, being, in either case, transmitted to Congress, and lodged among the acts of Congress, for the security of the parties concerned : Provided, that every commissioner, before he sits in judgment, shall take an oath, to be administered by one of the judges of the supreme or superior court of the State, where the cause shall be tried, 'Well and truly to hear and determine the matter in question, according to the best of his judgment, without favor, affection, or hope of reward' : Provided, also, that no State shall be deprived of territory for the benefit of the United States.

All controversies concerning the private right of soil claimed under different grants of two or more States, whose jurisdictions, as they may respect such lands, and the States which passed such grants are adjusted, the said grants or either of them being at the same time claimed to have originated antecedent to such settlement of jurisdiction, shall, on the petition of either party to the Congress of the United States, be finally determined, as near as may be, in the same manner as is before prescribed for deciding disputes respecting territorial jurisdiction between different States.

The United States, in Congress assembled, shall also have the sole and exclusive right and power of regulating the alloy and value of coin struck by their own authority, or by that of the respective States : Fixing the standard of weights and measures throughout the United States : Regulating the trade and managing all affairs with the Indians, not members of any of the States ; provided that the legislative right of any State, within its own limits, be not infringed or violated : Establishing and regulating post-offices from one State to another, throughout all the United States, and exacting such postage on the papers passing through the same as may be requisite to defray the expenses of the said office : Appointing all officers of the land forces in the service of the United States, excepting regimental officers : Appointing all the officers of the naval forces, and commissioning all officers whatever in the service of the United States : Making rules for the government and regulation of the land and naval forces, and directing their operations.

The United States in Congress assembled shall have authority to appoint a committee, to sit in the recess of Congress, to be denominated A COMMITTEE OF THE STATES, and to consist of one delegate from each State ; and to appoint such other committees and civil officers as may be necessary for managing the general affairs of the United States under their direction : To appoint one of their number to preside ; provided, that no person be allowed to serve in the office of President more than one year in any term of three years. To ascertain the necessary sums of money to be raised for the service of the United States, and to appropriate and apply the same for defraying the public expenses : To borrow money, or emit bills on the credit of the United States, transmitting every half year to the respective States an account of the sums of money so borrowed or emitted : To build and equip a navy : To agree upon the number of land forces, and to make requisitions from each State for its quota, in proportion to the number of white inhabitants in such State, which requisition shall be binding ; and thereupon the legislature of each State shall appoint the regimental officers, raise the men, and clothe, arm, and equip them, in a soldierlike manner, at the expense of the United States ; and the officers and men so clothed, armed, and equipped, shall march to the place appointed, and within the time agreed on, by the United States in Congress assembled : but if the United States in Congress assembled shall, on consideration of circumstances, judge proper that any State should not raise men, or should raise a smaller number than its quota, and that any other State should raise a greater number of men than its quota thereof, such extra number shall be raised, officered, clothed, armed, and equipped, in the same manner as the quota of such State ; unless the legislature of such State shall judge that such extra number cannot be safely spared out of the same ; in which case they shall raise, officer, clothe, arm, and equip, as many of such extra number as they judge can be safely spared ; and the officers and men so clothed, armed, and equipped, shall march to the place appointed, and within the time agreed on, by the United States in Congress assembled.

The United States in Congress assembled shall never engage in a war ; nor grant letters of marque and reprisal in time of peace, nor enter into any treaties or alliances, nor coin money, nor regulate the value thereof, nor ascertain the sums and expenses necessary for the defense and welfare of the United States, or any of them, nor emit bills, nor borrow money on the credit of the United States, nor appropriate money, nor agree upon the number of vessels of war to be built or purchased, or the number of land or sea forces to be raised, nor appoint a commander-in-chief of the army or navy, unless nine States assent to the same ; nor shall a question on any other point, except for adjourning from day to day, be determined, unless by the votes of a majority of the United States in Congress assembled.

The Congress of the United States shall have power to adjourn to any time within the year, and to any place within the United States, so that no period of adjournment be for a longer duration than the space of six months, and shall publish the journal of their proceedings monthly, except such parts thereof relating to treaties, alliances, or military operations as in their judgment require secrecy ; and the yeas and nays of the delegates of each State, on any question, shall be entered on the journal, when it is desired by any delegate ; and the delegates of a State, or any of them, at his or their request, shall be furnished with a transcript of the said journal, except such parts as are above excepted, to lay before the legislatures of the several States.

ARTICLE X.

The committee of the States, or any nine of them, shall be authorized to execute, in the recess of Congress, such of the powers of Congress as the United States in Congress assembled, by the consent of nine States, shall, from time to time, think expedient to vest them with ; provided that no power be delegated to the said committee, for the exercise of which, by the Articles of Confederation, the voice of nine States, in the Congress of the United States assembled, is requisite.

ARTICLE XI.

Canada, acceding to this Confederation, and joining in the measures of the United States, shall be admitted into and entitled to all the advantages of this Union ; but no other colony shall be admitted into the same unless such admission be agreed to by nine States.

ARTICLE XII.

All bills of credit emitted, moneys borrowed, and debts contracted by or under the authority of Congress, before the assembling of the United States, in pursuance of the present Confederation, shall be deemed and considered as a charge against the

United States, for payment and satisfaction whereof the said United States and the public faith are hereby solemnly pledged.

ARTICLE XIII.

Every State shall abide by the determinations of the United States in Congress assembled, on all questions which, by this Confederation, are submitted to them. And the Articles of this Confederation shall be inviolably observed by every State ; and the Union shall be perpetual. Nor shall any alteration at any time hereafter be made in any of them, unless such alteration be agreed to, in a Congress of the United States, and be afterward confirmed by the legislatures of every State.

And whereas, it has pleased the great Governor of the world to incline the hearts of the legislatures we respectively represent in Congress, to approve of, and to authorize us to ratify, the said Articles of Confederation and Perpetual Union :

KNOW YE, That we, the undersigned delegates, by virtue of the power and authority to us given for that purpose, do, by these presents, in the name, and in behalf, of our respective constituents, fully and entirely ratify and confirm each and every of the said Articles of Confederation and Perpetual Union, and all and singular the matters and things therein contained. And we do further solemnly plight and engage the faith of our respective constituents, that they shall abide by the determinations of the United States in Congress assembled, on all questions, which, by the said Confederation, are submitted to them ; and that the articles thereof shall be inviolably observed by the States we respectively represent ; and that the Union shall be perpetual.

In witness whereof, we have hereunto set our hands in Congress.

Done at Philadelphia, in the State of Pennsylvania, the ninth day of July, in the year of our Lord one thousand seven hundred and seventy-eight and in the third year of the Independence of America.

II

CONSTITUTION OF THE UNITED STATES OF AMERICA.

We, the People of the United States, in order to form a more perfect union, establish justice, insure domestic tranquility, provide for the common defence, promote the general welfare, and secure the blessings of liberty to ourselves and our posterity, do ordain and establish this Constitution for the United States of America.

ARTICLE I.

SECTION 1.

1. All Legislative powers herein granted, shall be vested in a Congress of the United States, which shall consist of a Senate and a House of Representatives.

SECTION 2.

1. The House of Representatives shall be composed of members chosen every second year by the people of the several States, and the electors in each State shall have the qualifications requisite for electors of the most numerous branch of the State legislature.

2. No person shall be a Representative who shall not have attained to the age of twenty-five years, and been seven years a citizen of the United States, and who shall not, when elected, be an inhabitant of that State in which he shall be chosen.

3. Representatives and direct taxes shall be apportioned among the several States which may be included within this Union, according to their respective numbers, which shall be determined by adding to the whole number of free persons, including those bound to service for a term of years, and excluding Indians not taxed, three-fifths of all other persons. The actual enumeration shall be made within three years after the first meeting of the Congress of the United States, and within every subsequent term of ten years, in such manner as they shall by law direct. The number of Representatives shall not exceed one for every thirty

thousand, but each State shall have at least one Representative ; and until such enumeration shall be made, the State of New Hampshire shall be entitled to choose three, Massachusetts eight, Rhode Island and Providence Plantations one, Connecticut five. New York six, New Jersey four, Pennsylvania eight, Delaware one, Maryland six, Virginia ten, North Carolina five, South Carolina five, and Georgia three.

4. When vacancies happen in the representation from any State, the executive authority thereof shall issue writs of election to fill such vacancies.

5. The House of Representatives shall choose their Speaker and other officers ; and shall have the sole power of impeachment.

SECTION 3.

1. The Senate of the United States shall be composed of two Senators from each State, chosen by the legislature thereof, for six years ; and each Senator shall have one vote.

2. Immediately after they shall be assembled in consequence of the first election, they shall be divided, as equally as may be, into three classes. The seats of the Senators of the first class shall be vacated at the expiration of the second year ; of the second class, at the expiration of the fourth year ; and of the third class, at the expiration of the sixth year ; so that one-third may be chosen every second year ; and if vacancies happen by resignation, or otherwise, during the recess of the legislature of any State. the executive thereof may make temporary appointments until the next meeting of the legislature, which shall then fill such vacancies.

3. No person shall be a Senator who shall not have attained to the age of thirty years, and been nine years a citizen of the United States, and who shall not, when elected, be an inhabitant of that State for which he shall be chosen.

4. The Vice-President of the United States shall be President of the Senate, but shall have no vote, unless they be equally divided.

5. The Senate shall choose their other officers, and also a President *pro tempore*, in the absence of the Vice-President, or when he shall exercise the office of President of the United States.

6. The Senate shall have the sole power to try all impeachments. When sitting for that purpose, they shall be on oath or

affirmation. When the President of the United States is tried, the Chief Justice shall preside, and no person shall be convicted without the concurrence of two-thirds of the members present.

7. Judgment in cases of impeachment shall not extend further than to removal from office, and disqualification to hold and enjoy any office of honor, trust, or profit, under the United States ; but the party convicted shall, nevertheless, be liable and subject to indictment, trial, judgment, and punishment, according to law.

SECTION 4.

1. The times, places, and manner, of holding elections for Senators and Representatives, shall be prescribed in each State by the legislature thereof ; but the Congress may at any time, by law, make or alter such regulations, except as to the places of choosing Senators.

2. The Congress shall assemble at least once in every year, and such meeting shall be on the first Monday in December, unless they shall by law appoint a different day.

SECTION 5.

1. Each House shall be the judge of the elections, returns, and qualifications, of its own members, and a majority of each shall constitute a quorum to do business : but a smaller number may adjourn from day to day, and may be authorized to compel the attendance of absent members, in such manner, and under such penalties, as each House may provide.

2. Each House may determine the rules of its proceedings, punish its members for disorderly behavior, and, with the concurrence of two-thirds, expel a member.

3. Each House shall keep a journal of its proceedings, and, from time to time, publish the same, excepting such parts as may in their judgment, require secrecy ; and the yeas and nays of the members of either House, on any question, shall, at the desire of one-fifth of those present, be entered on the journal.

4. Neither house, during the session of Congress, shall, without the consent of the other, adjourn for more than three days, nor to any other place than that in which the two Houses shall be sitting.

SECTION 6.

1. The Senators and Representatives shall receive a compensation for their services, to be ascertained by law, and paid out of

the Treasury of the United States. They shall in all cases, except treason, felony, and breach of the peace, be privileged from arrest during their attendance at the session of their respective Houses, and in going to, and returning from, the same ; and for any speech or debate in either House, they shall not be questioned in any other place.

2. No Senator or Representative shall, during the time for which he was elected, be appointed to any civil office under the authority of the United States, which shall have been created, or the emoluments whereof shall have been increased, during such time ; and no person, holding any office under the United States, shall be a member of either House during his continuance in office.

SECTION 7.

1. All bills for raising revenue shall originate in the House of Representatives ; but the Senate may propose or concur with amendments as on other bills.

2. Every bill which shall have passed the House of Representatives and the Senate, shall, before it becomes a law, be presented to the President of the United States ; if he approve, he shall sign it, but if not, he shall return it, with his objections, to that House in which it shall have originated, who shall enter the objections at large in their Journal, and proceed to reconsider it. If, after such reconsideration, two-thirds of that House shall agree to pass the bill, it shall be sent, together with the objections, to the other House, by which it shall likewise be reconsidered, and if approved by two-thirds of that House it shall become a law. But in all such cases the votes of both Houses shall be determined by yeas and nays, and the names of the persons voting for and against the bill shall be entered on the Journal of each House, respectively. If any bill shall not be returned by the President within ten days (Sundays excepted) after it shall have been presented to him, the same shall be a law, in like manner as if he had signed it, unless the Congress, by their adjournment, prevent its return, in which case it shall not be a law.

3. Every order, resolution or vote, to which the concurrence of the Senate and House of Representatives may be necessary (except on a question of adjournment), shall be presented to the President of the United States ; and before the same shall take

effect, shall be approved by him, or being disapproved by him, shall be re-passed by two-thirds of the Senate and House of Representatives, according to the rules and limitations prescribed in the case of a bill.

Section 8.

The Congress shall have power,—

1. To lay and collect taxes, duties, imposts, and excises, to pay the debts, and provide for the common defence and general welfare of the United States ; but all duties, imposts, and excises, shall be uniform thoughout the United States :

2. To borrow money on the credit of the United States :

3. To regulate commerce with foreign nations, and among the several States, and with the Indian tribes :

4. To establish a uniform rule of naturalization, and uniform laws on the subject of bankruptcies, throughout the United States :

5. To coin money, regulate the value thereof, and of foreign coin, and fix the standard of weights and measures :

6. To provide for the punishment of counterfeiting the securities and current coin of the United States :

7. To establish post-offices and post-roads :

8. To promote the progress of science and useful arts, by securing, for limited times, to authors and inventors, the exclusive right to their respective writings and discoveries :

9. To constitute tribunals inferior to the Supreme Court :

10. To define and punish piracies and felonies committed on the high seas, and offences against the law of nations :

11. To declare war, grant letters of marque and reprisal, and make rules concerning captures on land and water :

12. To raise and support armies ; but no appropriation of money to that use shall be for a longer term than two years :

13. To provide and maintain a navy :

14. To make rules for the government and regulation of the land and naval forces :

15. To provide for calling forth the militia to execute the laws of the Union, suppress insurrections, and repel invasions :

16. To provide for organizing, arming, and disciplining, the militia, and for governing such part of them as may be employed in the service of the United States, reserving to the States, respectively, the appointment of the officers, and the authority of training the militia, according to the discipline prescribed by Congress.

17. To exercise exclusive legislation, in all cases whatsoever, over such district (not exceeding ten miles square) as may, by cession of particular States, and the acceptance of Congress become the seat of the government of the United States, and to exercise like authority over all places, purchased by the consent of the legislature of the State in which the same shall be, for the erection of forts, magazines, arsenals, dock-yards, and other needful buildings : And,—

18. To make all laws which shall be necessary and proper for carrying into execution the foregoing powers, and all other powers vested by this Constitution in the Government of the United States, or in any department or officer thereof.

SECTION 9.

1. The migration or importation of such persons, as any of the States, now existing, shall think proper to admit, shall not be prohibited by the Congress prior to the year one thousand eight hundred and eight ; but a tax or duty may be imposed on such importation, not exceeding ten dollars for each person.

2. The privilege of the writ of *habeas corpus* shall not be suspended, unless when, in cases of rebellion or invasion, the public safety may require it.

3. No bill of attainder, or *ex post facto* law, shall be passed.

4. No capitation or other direct tax shall be laid, unless in proportion to the census or enumeration hereinbefore directed to be taken.

5. No tax or duty shall be laid on articles exported from any State. No preference shall be given by any regulation of commerce or revenue, to the ports of one State over those of another, nor shall vessels bound to, or from, one State, be obliged to enter, clear, or pay duties, in another.

6. No money shall be drawn from the treasury but in consequence of appropriations made by law, and a regular statement and account of the receipts and expenditures of all public money shall be published from time to time.

7. No title of nobility shall be granted by the United States ; and no person holding any office of profit or trust under them, shall, without the consent of the Congress, accept of any present, emolument, office, or title, of any kind whatever, from any king, prince, or foreign state.

SECTION 10.

1. No State shall enter into any treaty, alliance, or confederation; grant letters of marque and reprisal; coin money; emit bills of credit; make anything but gold and silver coin a tender in payment of debts; pass any bill of attainder, *ex post facto* law, or law impairing the obligation of contracts, or grant any title of nobility.

2. No State shall, without the consent of the Congress, lay any imposts or duties on imports or exports, except what may be absolutely necessary for executing its inspection laws; and the net produce of all duties and imposts laid by any State on imports or exports, shall be for the use of the treasury of the United States; and all such laws shall be subject to the revision and control of the Congress. No State shall, without the consent of Congress, lay any duty of tonnage, keep troops or ships of war in time of peace, enter into any agreement or compact with another State, or with a foreign power, or engage in war, unless actually invaded or in such imminent danger as will not admit of delay.

ARTICLE II.

SECTION 1.

1. The Executive power shall be vested in a President of the United States of America. He shall hold his office during the term of four years, and together with the Vice-President, chosen for the same term, be elected as follows:—

2. Each State shall appoint, in such manner as the Legislature thereof may direct, a number of Electors, equal to the whole number of Senators and Representatives to which the State may be entitled in the Congress; but no Senator or Representative, or person holding an office of trust or profit under the United States, shall be appointed an Elector.

Clause 3 has been superseded by the XIIth Article of Amendments, given under head of Amendments.

[3. The Electors shall meet in their respective States, and vote by ballot for two persons, of whom one, at least, shall not be an inhabitant of the same State with themselves. And they shall make a list of all the persons voted for, and of the number of votes for each; which list they shall sign and certify, and transmit, sealed, to the seat of the government of the United States, directed to the President of the Senate. The President of the Senate shall, in the presence of the Senate and House of Representatives, open all the certificates, and the votes shall then be counted. The person having the greatest number of votes shall be the President, if such number be a majority of the whole number of Electors appointed ; and if there be more than one who have such majority, and have an equal number of votes, then the House of Representatives shall immediately choose, by ballot, one of them for President; and if no person have a majority, then, from the five highest on the list, the said House shall, in like manner, choose the President. But in choosing the President, the votes shall be taken by States, the Representation from each State having one vote ; a quorum for this purpose shall consist of a member or members from two-thirds of the States, and a majority of all the States shall be necessary to a choice. In every case, after the choice of the President, the person having the greatest number of votes of the Electors shall be the Vice-President. But if there should remain two or more who have equal votes, the Senate shall choose from them, by ballot, the Vice-President.]

4. The Congress may determine the time of choosing the Electors, and the day on which they shall give their votes ; which day shall be the same throughout the United States.

5. No person, except a natural born citizen, or a citizen of the United States at the time of the adoption of this Constitution, shall be eligible to the office of President; neither shall any person be eligible to that office who shall not have attained to the age of thirty-five years, and been fourteen years a resident within the United States.

6. In case of the removal of the President from office, or of his death, resignation, or inability to discharge the powers and duties of the said office, the same shall devolve on the Vice-President, and the Congress may by law provide for the case of removal, death, resignation, or inability, both of the President and Vice-President, declaring what officer shall then act as President, and such officer shall act accordingly, until the disability be removed, or a President shall be elected.

7. The President shall, at stated times, receive for his services a compensation, which shall neither be increased nor diminished during the period for which he shall have been elected, and

he shall not receive within that period any other emolument from the United States or any of them.

8.   Before he enter on the execution of his office he shall take the following oath or affirmation :—

"I do solemnly swear (or affirm) that I will faithfully execute the office of President of the United States, and will, to the best of my ability, preserve, protect, and defend, the Constitution of the United States.

Section 2.

1.   The President shall be commander-in-chief of the army and navy of the United States, and of the militia of the several States when called into the actual service of the United States ; he may require the opinion, in writing, of the principal officer in each of the executive departments, upon any subject relating to the duties of their respective offices, and he shall have power to grant reprieves and pardons for offences against the United States except in cases of impeachment.

2.   He shall have power, by and with the advice and consent of the Senate, to make treaties, provided two-thirds of the Senators present concur ; and he shall nominate, and by and with the advice and consent of the Senate, shall appoint ambassadors, other public ministers, and consuls, judges of the Supreme Court, and all other officers of· the United States, whose appointments are not herein otherwise provided for, and which shall be established by law ; but the Congress may by law vest the appointment of such inferior officers, as they think proper, in the President alone, in the courts of law, or in the heads of Departments.

3.   The President shall have power to fill up all vacancies that may happen, during the recess of the Senate, by granting commissions, which shall expire at the end of their next session.

Section 3.

He shall, from time to time, give to the Congress information of the state of the Union, and recommend to their consideration such measures as he shall judge necessary and expedient ; he may, on extraordinary occasions, convene both Houses, or either of them, and in case of disagreement between them with respect to the time of adjournment, he may adjourn them to such time as he shall think proper ; he shall receive ambassadors and other public ministers ; he shall take care that the laws be faithfully executed, and shall commission all the officers of the United States.

SECTION 4.

The President, Vice-President, and all civil officers of the United States, shall be removed from office on impeachment for, and conviction of, treason, bribery, or other high crimes and misdemeanors.

ARTICLE III.

SECTION 1.

The Judicial power of the United States shall be vested in one Supreme Court, and in such inferior courts as the Congress may, from time to time, ordain and establish. The judges, both of the Supreme and inferior courts, shall hold their offices during good behavior, and shall, at stated times, receive for their services a compensation, which shall not be diminished during their continuance in office.

SECTION 2.

1. The Judicial power shall extend to all cases, in law and equity, arising under this Constitution, the laws of the United States, and treaties made, or which shall be made, under their authority; to all cases affecting embassadors, other public ministers, and consuls; to all cases of admiralty and maritime jurisdiction; to controversies to which the United States shall be a party; to controversies between two or more States, between a State and citizens of another State, between citizens of different States, between citizens of the same State claiming lands under grants of different States, and between a State, or the citizens thereof, and foreign States, citizens, or subjects.

2. In all cases affecting embassadors, other public ministers, and consuls, and those in which a State shall be a party, the Supreme Court shall have original jurisdiction. In all the other cases before mentioned, the Supreme Court shall have appellate jurisdiction, both as to law and fact, with such exceptions, and under such regulations, as the Congress shall make.

3. The trial of all crimes, except in cases of impeachment, shall be by jury; and such trial shall be held in the State where the said crimes shall have been committed; but when not committed within any State, the trial shall be at such place, or places, as the Congress may by law have directed.

SECTION 3.

1. Treason against the United States shall consist only in levying war against them, or in adhering to their enemies, giving them aid and comfort. No person shall be convicted of treason, unless on the testimony of two witnesses to the same overt act, or on confession in open court.

2. The Congress shall have power to declare the punishment of treason, but no attainder of treason shall work corruption of blood, or forfeiture, except during the life of the person attained.

ARTICLE IV.

SECTION 1.

Full faith and credit shall be given in each State to the public acts, records, and judicial proceedings of every other State. And the Congress may, by general laws, prescribe the manner in which such acts, records, and proceedings shall be proved, and the effect thereof.

SECTION 2.

1. The citizens of each State shall be entitled to all privileges and immunities of citizens in the several States.

2. A person charged in any State with treason, felony, or other crime, who shall flee from justice, and be found in another State, shall, on demand of the Executive authority of the State from which he fled, be delivered up, to be removed to the State having jurisdiction of the crime.

3. No person held to service or labor in one State, under the laws thereof, escaping into another, shall, in consequence of any law or regulation therein, be discharged from such service or labor, but shall be delivered up on claim of the party to whom such service or labor may be due.

SECTION 3.

1. New States may be admitted by the Congress into this Union ; but no new State shall be formed or erected within the jurisdiction of any other State ; nor any State be formed by the junction of two or more States, or parts of States, without the consent of the legislatures of the States concerned as well as of the Congress.

2. The Congress shall have power to dispose of and make all needful rules and regulations respecting the territory or other property belonging to the United States; and nothing in this Constitution shall be so construed as to prejudice any claims of the United States, or of any particular State.

SECTION 4.

The United States shall guarantee to every State in this Union a republican form of Government, and shall protect each of them against invasion; and, on application of the Legislature, or of the Executive (when the Legislature cannot be convened), against domestic violence.

ARTICLE V.

The Congress, whenever two-thirds of both Houses shall deem it necessary, shall propose Amendments to this Constitution, or, on the application of the legislatures of two-thirds of the several States, shall call a convention for proposing Amendments, which, in either case, shall be valid to all intents and purposes as part of this Constitution, when ratified by the legislatures of three-fourths of the several States, or by conventions in three-fourths thereof, as the one or the other mode of ratification may be proposed by the Congress: Provided, that no Amendment which may be made prior to the year one thousand eight hundred and eight shall in any manner affect the first and fourth clauses in the ninth section of the first article; and that no State, without its consent, shall be deprived of its equal suffrage in the Senate.

ARTICLE VI.

1. All debts contracted and engagements entered into, before the adoption of this Constitution, shall be as valid against the United States under this Constitution as under the Confederation.

2. This Constitution, and the laws of the United States which shall be made in pursuance thereof, and all treaties made, or which shall be made, under the authority of the United States, shall be the supreme law of the land; and the judges in every State shall be bound thereby, anything in the constitution or laws of any State to the contrary notwithstanding.

3. The Senators and Representatives before mentioned, and the members of the several State legislatures, and all executive

and judicial officers, both of the United States and of the several States, shall be bound by oath, or affirmation, to support this Constitution ; but no religious test shall ever be required as a qualification to any office or public trust under the United States.

ARTICLE VII.

The ratification of the Convention of nine States shall be sufficient for the establishment of this Constitution between the States so ratifying the same.

AMENDMENTS TO THE CONSTITUTION.

ARTICLE I.

Congress shall make no law respecting an establishment of religion, or prohibiting the free exercise thereof ; or abridging the freedom of speech or of the press ; or the right of the people peaceably to assemble and to petition the Government for a redress of grievances.

ARTICLE II.

A well regulated militia being necessary to the security of a free state, the right of the people to keep and bear arms shall not be infringed.

ARTICLE III.

No soldier shall, in time of peace, be quartered in any house without the consent of the owner ; nor in time of war, but in a manner to be prescribed by law.

ARTICLE IV.

The right of the people to be secure in their persons, houses, papers, and effects, against unreasonable searches and seizures, shall not be violated, and no warrants shall issue but upon probable cause, supported by oath or affirmation, and particularly describing the place to be searched, and the persons or things to be seized.

ARTICLE V.

No persons shall be held to answer for a capital or otherwise infamous crime, unless on a presentment or indictment of a grand jury, except in cases arising in the land or naval forces, or in the militia when in actual service in time of war or public danger; nor shall any person be subject for the same offence to be twice put in jeopardy of life or limb; nor shall be compelled in any criminal case to be a witness against himself; nor be deprived of life, liberty, or property, without due process of law; nor shall private property be taken for public use without just compensation.

ARTICLE VI.

In all criminal prosecutions the accused shall enjoy the right to a speedy and public trial, by an impartial jury of the State and district wherein the crime shall have been committed, which district shall have been previously ascertained by law, and to be informed of the nature and cause of the accusation; to be confronted with the witnesses against him; to have compulsory process for obtaining witnesses in his favor, and to have the assistance of counsel for his defense.

ARTICLE VII.

In suits at common law, where the value in controversy shall exceed twenty dollars, the right of trial by jury shall be preserved, and no fact tried by a jury shall be otherwise re-examined in any Court of the United States than according to the rules of the common law.

ARTICLE VIII.

Excessive bail shall not be required, nor excessive fines imposed, nor cruel and unusual punishments inflicted.

ARTICLE IX.

The enumeration in the Constitution of certain rights shall not be construed to deny or disparage others retained by the people.

ARTICLE X.

The powers not delegated to the United States by the Constitution, nor prohibited by it to the States, are reserved to the States respectively, or to the people.

ARTICLE XI.

The judicial power of the United States shall not be construed to extend to any suit in law or equity commenced or prosecuted against one of the United States by citizens of another State, or by citizens or subjects of any foreign State.

ARTICLE XII.

The Electors shall meet in their respective States, and vote by ballot for President and Vice-President, one of whom, at least, shall not be an inhabitant of the same State with themselves; they shall name in their ballots the person voted for as President, and in distinct ballots the person voted for as Vice-President, and they shall make distinct lists of all persons voted for as President, and of all persons voted for as Vice-President, and of the number of votes for each, which lists they shall sign and certify, and transmit sealed to the seat of the government of the United States directed to the President of the Senate. The President of the Senate shall, in the presence of the Senate and House of Representatives, open all the certificates, and the votes shall then be counted; the person having the greatest number of votes for President shall be the President, if such number be a majority of the whole number of electors appointed; and if no person have such majority, then from the persons having the highest numbers, not exceeding three, on the list of those voted for as President, the House of Representatives shall choose immediately, by ballot, the President. But in choosing the President, the votes shall be taken by States, the representation from each State having one vote; a quorum for this purpose shall consist of a member or members from two-thirds of the States, and a majority of all the States shall be necessary to a choice. And if the House of Representatives shall not choose a President, whenever the right of choice shall devolve upon them, before the fourth day of March next following, then the Vice-President shall act as President, as in the case of the death or other constitutional disability of the President. The person having the greatest number of votes as Vice-President shall be the Vice-President, if such number be a majority of the whole number of electors appointed, and if no person have a majority, then from the two highest numbers on the list the Senate shall choose the Vice-President; a quorum for the purpose shall consist of two-thirds of the whole number of Senators, and a majority of the whole number shall be necessary to a choice. But no person constitutionally ineligible to the office of President shall be eligible to that of Vice-President of the United States.

ARTICLE XIII.

1. Neither slavery nor involuntary servitude, except as a punishment for crime, whereof the party shall have been duly convicted, shall exist within the United States, or any place subject to their jurisdiction.

2. The Congress shall have power to enforce this article by appropriate legislation.

ARTICLE XIV.

1. All persons born or naturalized in the United States, and subject to the jurisdiction thereof, are citizens of the United States and of the State wherein they reside. No State shall make or enforce any law which shall abridge the privileges or immunities of citizens of the United States ; nor shall any State deprive any person of life, liberty, or property, without due process of law, nor deny to any person within its jurisdiction the equal protection of the laws.

2. Representatives shall be apportioned among the several States according to their respective numbers, counting the whole number of persons in each State, excluding Indians not taxed. But when the right to vote at any election for the choice of electors for President and Vice-President of the United States, Representatives in the Congress, the Executive and Judicial officers of a State, or the members of the Legislature thereof, is denied to any of the male inhabitants of such State, being twenty-one years of age and citizens of the United States, or in any way abridged, except for participation in rebellion or other crime, the basis of representation therein shall be reduced in the proportion which the number of such male citizens shall bear to the whole number of male citizens twenty-one years of age in such State.

4. No person shall be a Senator or Representative in the Congress, or Elector of President and Vice-President, or hold any office, civil or military, under the United States, or under any State, who, having previously taken an oath, as a member of the Congress, or as an officer of the United States, or as a member of any State legislature, or as an executive or judicial officer of any State, to support the Constitution of the United States, shall have engaged in insurrection or rebellion against the same or given aid or comfort to the enemies thereof. But the Congress may, by a vote of two-thirds of each House, remove such disability.

4.   The validity of the public debt of the United States, author-ized by law, including debts incurred for payment of pensions and bounties for services in suppressing insurrection or rebellion, shall not be questioned.   But neither the United States nor any State shall assume or pay any debt or obligation incurred in aid of insurrection or rebellion against the United States, or any claim for the loss or emancipation of any slave ; but all such debts, obligations, and claims shall be held illegal and void.

5.   The Congress shall have power to enforce, by appropriate legislation, the provisions of this article.

ARTICLE XV.

1.   The right of citizens of the United States to vote shall not be denied or abridged by the United States, or by any State, on account of race, color, or previous condition of servitude.

3.   The Congress shall have power to enforce this article by appropriate legislation.

III.

KIN BEYOND SEA:

A COMPARISON OF THE ENGLISH AND AMERICAN CONSTITUTIONS BY W. E. GLADSTONE.

[FROM THE NORTH AMERICAN REVIEW, SEPT. 1878.]

1. IT is now nearly half a century since the works of De Tocqueville and De Beaumont, founded upon personal observation, brought the institutions of the United States effectually within the circle of European thought and interest. They were co-operators, but not upon an equal scale. De Beaumont belongs to the class of ordinary, though able, writers: De Tocqueville was the Burke of his age, and his treatise upon America may well be regarded as among the best books hitherto produced for the political student of all times and countries.

2. But higher and deeper than the concern of the old world at large in the thirteen colonies, now grown into thirty-eight States, besides eight Territories, is the special interest of England in their condition and prospects.

I do not speak of political controversies between them and us, which are happily, as I trust, at an end. I do not speak of the vast contribution, which, from year to year, through the operations of a colossal trade, each makes to the wealth and comfort of the other: nor of the friendly controversy, which in its own place it might be well to raise, between the leanings of America to Protectionism, and the more daring reliance of the old country upon free and unrestricted intercourse with all the world. Nor of the menace which, in the prospective development of her resources, America offers to the commercial pre-eminence of England.*

---

* [This topic was much more largely handled by me in the Financial Statement which I delivered as Chancellor of the Exchequer, on May 2, 1866. I recommend attention to the excellent article by Mr. Henderson, in the *Contemporary Review* for October, 1878: and I agree with the author in being disposed to think that the protective laws of America effectually bar the full development of her competing power.—W. E. G., Nov. 6, 1878.]

On this subject I will only say that it is she alone who, at a
coming time, can, and probably will, wrest from us that commercial primacy.   We have no title, I have no inclination, to murmer
at the prospect.   If she acquires it, she will make the acquisition
by the right of the strongest; but, in this instance, the strongest
means the best.   She will probably become what we are now,
the head servant in the great household of the World, the em-
ployer of all employed; because her service will be the most
and ablest.   We have no more title against her, than Venice, or
Genoa, or Holland has had against us.   One great duty is en-
tailed upon us, which we unfortunately neglect; the duty of pre-
paring, by a resolute and sturdy effort, to reduce our public
burdens, in preparation for a day when we shall probably have
less capacity than we have now to bear them.

3.   Passing by all these subjects, with their varied attractions,
I come to another, which lies within the tranquil domain of political philosophy.   The students of the future, in this department,
will have much to say in the way of comparison between American and British institutions.   The relationship between these two
is unique in history.   It is always interesting to trace and to compare Constitutions, as it is to compare languages; especially in
such instances as those of the Greek States and the Italian Repub-
lics, or the diversified forms of the feudal system in the different
countries of Europe.   But there is no parallel in all the records
of the world to the case of that prolific British mother, who has
sent forth her innumerable children over all the earth to be the
founders of a half-a-dozen empires.   She, with her progeny, may
almost claim to constitute a kind of Universal Church in politics.
But, among these children, there is one whose place in the world's
eye and in history is superlative: it is the American Republic.
She is the eldest born.   She has, taking the capacity of her land
into view as well as its mere measurement, a natural base for the
greatest continuous empire ever established by man.   And it may
be well here to mention what has not always been sufficiently
observed, that the distinction between continuous empire, and
empire severed and dispersed over sea, is vital.   The development, which the Republic has effected, has been unexampled in its
rapidity and force.   While other countries have doubled, or at
most trebled, their population, she has risen, during one single
century of freedom, in round numbers, from two millions to forty-

five. As to riches, it is reasonable to establish, from the decennial stages of the progress thus far achieved, a series for the future ; and reckoning upon this basis, I suppose that the very next Census, in the year 1880, will exhibit her to the world as certainly the wealthiest of all the nations. The huge figure of a thousand millions sterling, which may be taken roundly as the annual income of the United Kingdom, has been reached at a surprising rate ; a rate which may perhaps be best expressed by saying that, if we could have started forty or fifty years ago from zero, at the rate of our recent annual increment, we should now have reached our present position. But while we have been advancing with this portentious rapidity, America is passing us by as if in a canter. Yet even now the work of searching the soil and the bowels of the territory, and opening out her enterprise throughout its vast expanse, is in its infancy. The England and the America of the present are probably the two strongest nations of the world. But there can hardly be a doubt, as between the America and the England of the future, that the daughter, at some no very distant time, will, whether fairer or less fair, be unquestionably yet stronger than the mother.

" O matre forti filia fortior."*

4. But all this pompous detail of material triumphs, whether for the one or for the other, is worse than idle, unless the men of the two countries shall remain, or shall become, greater than the mere things that they produce, and shall know how to regard those things simply as tools and materials for the attainments of the highest purposes of their being. Ascending, then, from the ground floor of material industry towards the regions in which these purposes are to be wrought out, it is for each nation to consider how far its institutions have reached a state in which they can contribute their maximum to the store of human happiness and excellence. And for the political student all over the world, it will be beyond anything curious as well as useful to examine, with what diversities, as well as what resemblances, of apparatus, the two greater branches of a race born to command have been minded, or induced, or constrained to work out, in their sea-severed seats, their political destinies according to the respective laws appointed for them.

---

* See Hor. Od. I, 16.

No higher ambition can find vent in a paper such as this, than to suggest the position and claims of the subject, and slightly to indicate a few outlines, or at least, fragments, of the working material.

5. In many and the most fundamental respects the two still carry in undiminished, perhaps in increasing, clearness, the notes of resemblance that beseem a parent and a child.

Both wish for self-government; and, however grave the drawbacks under which in one or both it exists, the two have, among the great nations of the world, made the most effectual advances towards the true aim of rational politics.

They are similarly associated in their fixed idea that the force, in which all government takes effect, is to be constantly backed, and, as it were, illuminated by thought in speech and writing. The ruler of St. Paul's time "bare the sword" (Rom. xiii. 4). Bare it, as the Apostle says, with a mission to do right; but he says nothing of any duty, or any custom, to show by reason that he was doing right. Our two governments, whatsoever they do, have to give reasons for it; not reasons which will convince the unreasonable, but reasons which on the whole will convince the average mind, and carry it unitedly forwards in a course of action, often, though not always wise, and carrying within itself provisions, where it is unwise, for the correction of its own unwisdom before it grow into an intolerable rankness. They are governments, not of force only, but of persuasion.

6. Many more are the concords, and not less vital than these, of the two nations, as expressed in their institutions. They alike prefer the practical to the abstract. They tolerate opinion, with only a reserve on behalf of decency; and they desire to confine coercion to the province of action, and to leave thought, as such, entirely free. They set a high value on liberty for its own sake. They desire to give full scope to the principles of self-reliance in the people, and they deem self-help to be immeasurably superior to help in any other form; to be the only help, in short, which ought not to be continually, or periodically, put upon its trial, and required to make good its title. They mistrust and mislike the centralisation of power; and they cherish municipal, local, even parochial liberties, as nursery grounds, not only for the production here and there of able men, but for the general training of public virtue and independent spirit. They regard publicity as the vital

air of politics ; through which alone, in its freest circulation, opinions can be thrown into common stock for the good of all, and the
balance of relative rights and claims can be habitually and peaceably adjusted. It would be difficult in the case of any other pair
of nations, to present an assemblage of traits at once so common
and so distinctive, as has been given in this probably imperfect
enumeration.

7. There were, however, the strongest reasons why America
could not grow into a reflection or repetition of England. Passing
from a narrow island to a continent almost without bounds, the
colonists at once and vitally altered their conditions of thought,
as well as of existence, in relation to the most important and
most operative of all social facts, the possession of the soil. In
England, inequality lies imbedded in the very base of the social
structure ; in America it is a late, incidental, unrecognized product, not of tradition, but of industry and wealth, as they advance
with various and, of necessity, unequal steps. Heredity, seated
as an idea in the heart's core of Englishmen, and sustaining far
more than it is sustained by those of our institutions which
express it, was as truly absent from the intellectual and moral
store, with which the colonists traversed the Atlantic, as if it had
been some forgotten article in the bills of lading that made up
their cargoes. Equality combined with liberty, and renewable at
each descent from one generation to another, like a lease with
stipulated breaks, was the groundwork of their social creed. In
vain was it sought, by arrangements such as those connected with
the name of Baltimore or of Penn, to qualify the action of those
overpowering forces which so determined the case. Slavery
itself, strange as it now may seem, failed to impair the theory
however it may have imported into the practice a hideous solecism.
No hardier republicanism was generated in New England than in
the Slave States of the South, which produced so many of the
great statesmen of America.

8. It may be said that the North, and not the South, had the
larger number of colonists ; and was the centre of those commanding moral influences which gave to the country as a whole its
political and moral atmosphere. The type and form of manhood
for America was supplied neither by the Recusant in Maryland,
nor by the Cavalier in Virginia, but by the Puritan of New England ; and it would have been a form and type widely different

could the colonization have taken place a couple of centuries, or a
single century, sooner. Neither the Tudor, nor even the Plan-
tagenet period, could have supplied its special form. The Reformation was a cardinal factor in its production ; and this in more
ways than one.

9. Before that great epoch, the political forces of the country
were represented on the whole by the Monarch on one side, and
the people on the other. In the people, setting aside the latent
vein of Lollardism, there was a general homogeneity with respect
to all that concerned the relation of governors and governed. In
the deposition of Sovereigns, the resistance to abuses, the establishment of institutions for the defence of liberty, there were no two
parties to divide the land. But, with the Reformation a new
dualism was sensibly developed among us. Not a dualism so vio-
lent as to break up the national unity, but yet one so marked and
substantial that thenceforward it was very difficult for any individual or body of men to represent the entire English character,
and the old balance of its forces. The wrench which severed
the Church and people from the Roman obedience left for domestic settlement thereafter a tremendous internal question, between
the historical and the new, which in its milder form perplexes us
to this day. Except during the short reign of Edward VI, the
civil power, in various methods and degrees, took what may be
termed the traditionary side, and favoured the development of the
historical more than the individual aspect of the national religion.
These elements confronted one another during the reigns of the
earlier Stuarts, not only with obstinacy but with fierceness.
There had grown up with the Tudors, from a variety of causes, a
great exaggeration of the idea of Royal power ; and this arrived,
under James I and Charles I, at a rank maturity. Not less, but
even more masculine and determined, was the converse development. Mr. Hallam saw, and has said, that at the outbreak of the
Great Rebellion, the old British Constitution was in danger, not
from one party but from both. In that mixed fabric had once
been harmonised the ideas, both of religious duty, and of allegiance as related to it, which were now held in severance. The
hardiest and dominating portion of the American Colonists represented that severance in its extremest form and had dropped out
of the order of the ideas, which they carried across the water, all
those elements of political Anglicism, which give to aristocracy

in this country a position only second in strength to that of freedom. State and Church alike had frowned upon them; and their
strong reaction was a reaction of their entire nature, alike of the
spiritual and the secular man. All that was democratic in the
policy of England, and all that was Protestant in her religion, they
carried with them, in pronounced and exclusive forms, to a soil
and a scene singularly suited for their growth.

10. It is to the honour of the British Monarchy that, upon the
whole, it frankly recognised the facts, and did not pedantically
endeavour to constrain by artificial and alien limitations the growth
of the infant States. It is a thing to be remembered that the
accusations of the colonies in 1776 were entirely levelled at the
King actually on the throne, and that a general acquittal was thus
given by them to every preceding reign. Their infancy had been
upon the whole what their manhood was to be, self-governed and
republican. Their Revolution, as we call it, was like ours in the
main, a vindication of liberties inherited and possessed. It was
a Conservative revolution; and the happy result was that, notwithstanding the sharpness of the collision with the mother-country,
and with domestic loyalism, the Thirteen Colonies made provision
for their future in conformity, as to all that determined life and
manners, with the recollections of their past. The two Constitutions of the two countries express indeed rather the differences
than the resemblances of the nations. The one is a thing grown,
the other a thing made : the one a *praxis*, the other a *poiesis :* the
one the offspring of tendency and intermediate time, the other of
choice and of an epoch. But, as the British Constitution is the
most subtle organism which has proceeded from the womb and the
long gestation of progressive history, so the American Constitution
is, so far as I can see, the most wonderful work ever struck off at
a given time by the brain and purpose of man. It has had a
century of trial, under the pressure of exigencies caused by an
expansion unexampled in point of rapidity and range : and its
exemption from formal change, though not entire, has certainly
proved the sagacity of the constructors, and the stubborn strength
of the fabric.

11. One whose life has been greatly absorbed in working, with
others, the institutions of his own country, has not had the opportunities necessary for the careful and searching scrutiny of institutions elsewhere. I should feel, in looking at those of America,

like one who attempts to scan the stars with the naked eye. My notices can only be few, faint, and superficial; they are but an introduction to what I have to say of the land of my birth. A few sentences will dispose of them.

12. America, whose attitude towards England has always been masculine and real, has no longer to anticipate at our hands the frivolous and offensive criticisms which were once in vogue among us. But neither nation prefers (and it would be an ill sign if either did prefer) the institutions of the other; and we certainly do not contemplate the great Republic in the spirit of mere optimism. We see that it has a marvellous and unexampled adaptation for its peculiar vocation; that it must be judged, not in the abstract, but under the fore-ordered laws of its existence; that it has purged away the blot with which we brought it into the world; that it bravely and vigorously grapples with the problem of making a Continent into a State; and that it treasures with fondness the traditions of British antiquity, which are in truth unconditionally its own, as well, and as much as they are ours. The thing that perhaps chiefly puzzles the inhabitants of the old country is why the American people should permit their entire existence to be continually disturbed by the business of the Presidential elections; and, still more, why they should raise to its maximum the intensity of this perturbation by providing, as we are told, for what is termed a clean sweep of the entire Civil Service, in all its ranks and departments, on each accession of a Chief Magistrate. We do not perceive why this arrangement is more rational than would be a corresponding usage in this country on each change of Ministry. Our practice is as different as possible. We limit to a few scores of persons the removals and appointments on these occasions; although our Ministries seem to us, not unfrequently, to be more sharply severed from one another in principle and tendency than are the successive Presidents of the great Union.

13. It would be out of place to discuss in this article occasional phenomena of local corruption in the United States, by which the nation at large can hardly be touched: or the mysterious manipulations of votes for the Presidency, which are now understood to be under examination; or the very curious influences which are shaping the politics of the negroes and of the South. These last are corollaries to the great slave-question; and it seems very possible that after a few years we may see most of the labourers, both

in the Southern States and in England, actively addicted to the
political support of that section of their countrymen who to the
last had resisted their emancipation.

14. But if there be those in this country who think that American democracy means public levity and intemperance, or a lack of
skill and sagacity in politics, or the absence of self-command and
self-denial, let them bear in mind a few of the most salient and
recent facts of history which may profitably be recommended to
their reflections. We emancipated a million of negroes by peace-
ful legislation ; America liberated four or five millions by a bloody
civil war : yet the industry and exports of the Southern States are
maintained, while those of our negro colonies have dwindled ; the
South enjoys all its franchises, but we have *proh pudor !* found no
better method of providing for peace and order in Jamaica, the
chief of our islands, than by the hard and vulgar, even where needful, expedient of abolishing entirely its representative institutions.

15. The Civil War compelled the States, both North and South,
to train and embody a million and a half of men, and to present
to view the greatest, instead of the smallest, armed forces in the
world. Here there was supposed to arise a double danger. First
that, on a sudden cessation of the war, military life and habits
could not be shaken off, and, having become rudely and widely
predominant, would bias the country towards an aggressive policy,
or, still worse, would find vent in predatory or revolutionary operations. Secondly, that a military caste would grow up with its
habits of exclusiveness and command, and would influence the
tone of politics in a direction adverse to republican freedom. But
both apprehensions proved to be wholly imaginary. The innumerable soldiery was at once dissolved. Cincinnatus, no longer
an unique example, became the commonplace of every day, the
type and mould of a nation. The whole enormous mass quietly
resumed the habits of social life. The generals of yesterday were
the editors, the secretaries, and the solicitors of to-day. The
just jealousy of the State gave life to the now forgotten maxim of
Judge Blackstone, who denounced as perilous the erection of a
separate profession of arms in a free country. The standing
army, expanded by the heat of civil contest to gigantic dimensions, settled down again into the framework of a miniature with
the returning temperature of civil life, and became a power well
nigh invisible, from its minuteness, amidst the powers which sway
the movements of a society exceeding forty millions.

16. More remarkable still was the financial sequel to the great conflict. The internal taxation for federal purposes, which before its commencement had been unknown, was raised, in obedience to an exigency of life and death, so as to exceed every present and every past example. It pursued and worried all the transactions of life. The interest of the American debt grew to be the highest in the world, and the capital touched five hundred and sixty millions sterling. Here was provided for the faith and patience of the people a touchstone of extreme severity. In England, at the close of the great French war, the propertied classes, who were supreme in Parliament, at once rebelled against the Tory Government, and refused to prolong the Income Tax even for a single year. We talked big, both then and now, about the payment of our National Debt ; but sixty-three years have since elapsed, all of them except two called years of peace, and we have reduced the huge total by about one-ninth ; that is to say, by little over one hundred millions, or scarcely more than one million and a half a year. This is the conduct of a State elaborately digested into orders and degrees, famed for wisdom and forethought, and consolidated by a long experience. But America continued long to bear, on her unaccustomed and still smarting shoulders, the burden of the war taxation. In twelve years she has reduced her debt by one hundred and fifty-eight millions sterling, or at the rate of thirteen millions for every year. In each twelve months she has done what we did in eight years ; her self-command, self-denial, and wise forethought for the future have been, to say the least, eight-fold ours. These are facts which redound greatly to her honour ; and the historian will record with surprise that an enfranchised nation tolerated burdens which in this country a selected class, possessed of the representation, did not dare to face, and that the most unmitigated democracy known to the annals of the world resolutely reduced at its own cost prospective liabilities of the State, which the aristocratic, and plutocratic, and Monarchical Government of the United Kingdom has been contented ignobly to hand over to posterity. And such facts should be told out. It is our fashion so to tell them, against as well as for ourselves ; and the record of them may some day be among the means of stirring us up to a policy more worthy of the name and fame of England.

17. It is true, indeed, that we lie under some heavy and, I fear, increasing disadvantages, which amount almost to disabili-

ties. Not, however, any disadvantage respecting power, as power is commonly understood. But, while America has a nearly homogeneous country, and an admirable division of political labour between the States individually and the Federal Government, we are, in public affairs, an overcharged and overweighted people.*

We have undertaken the cares of Empire upon a scale, and with a diversity, unexampled in history ; and, as it has not yet pleased Providence to endow us with brainforce and animal strength in an equally abnormal proportion, the consequence is that we perform the work of government, as to many among its more important departments, in a very superficial and slovenly manner. The affairs of the three associated Kingdoms, with their great diversities of law, interest, and circumstance, make the government of them, even if they stood alone, a business more voluminous, so to speak, than that of any other thirty-three millions of civilized men. To lighten the cares of the central legislature by judicious devolution, it is probable that much might be done ; but nothing is done, or even attempted to be done. The greater Colonies have happily attained to a virtual self-government ; yet the aggregate mass of business connected with our colonial possessions continues to be very large. The Indian Empire is of itself a charge so vast, and demanding so much thought and care, that if it were the sole transmarine appendage to the Crown, it would amply tax the best ordinary stock of human energies. Notoriously, it obtains from the Parliament only a small fraction of the attention it deserves. Questions affecting individuals, again, or small interests, or classes, excite here a greater interest, and occupy a larger share of time, than, perhaps, in any other community. In no country, I may add, are the interests of persons or classes so favoured when they compete with those of the public ; and in none are they more exacting, or more wakeful to turn this advantage to the best account. With the vast extension of our enterprise and our trade, comes a breadth of liability not less large, to consider everything that is critical in the affairs of foreign States ; and the real responsibilities, thus ex-

---

* [This subject has been more fully developed by me in an article on 'England's Mission,' contributed to *The Nineteenth Century* for September of the present year.— W. E. G., December 1878.]

isting for us, are unnaturally inflated by fast-growing tendencies
towards exaggeration of our concern in these matters, and even
towards setting up fictitious interests in cases where none can
discern them except ourselves, and such Continental friends as
practise upon our credulity and our fears for purposes of their
own. Last of all, it is not to be denied that in what I have been
saying, I do not represent the public sentiment. The nation is
not at all conscious of being overdone. The people see that their
House of Commons is the hardest-working legislative assembly in
the world : and, this being so, they assume it is all right. Nothing pays better, in point of popularity, than those gratuitous additions to obligations already beyond human strength, which look
like accessions or assertion of power ; such as the annexation of
new territory, or the silly transaction known as the purchase
of shares in the Suez Canal.

18.   All my life long I have seen this excess of work as compared with the power to do it ; but the evil has increased with the
surfeit of wealth, and there is no sign that the increase is near its
end. The people of this country are a very strong people ; but
there is no strength that can permanently endure, without provok-
ing inconvenient consequences, this kind of political debauch. It
may be hoped, but it cannot be predicted, that the mischief will be
encountered and subdued at the point where it will have become
sensibly troublesome, but will not have grown to be quite irremediable.   •

19.   The main and central point of interest, however, in the institutions of a country is the manner in which it draws together
and compounds the public forces in the balanced action of the
State. It seems plain that the formal arrangements for this purpose in America are very different from ours. It may even be a
question whether they are not, in certain respects, less popular ;
whether our institutions do not give more rapid effect, than those
of the Union, to any formed opinion. and resolved intention, of the
nation.

20.   In the formation of the Federal government we seem to
perceive three stages of distinct advancement. First, the formation of the Confederation, under the pressure of the War of Independence. Secondly, the Constitution, which placed the Federal
Goverment in defined and direct relation with the people inhabiting
the several States. Thirdly, the struggle with the South, which

for the first time, and definitely, decided that to the Union, through its Federal organisation, and not to the State-governments, were reserved all the questions not decided and disposed of by the express provisions of the Constitution itself.* The great *arcanum imperii*, which with us belongs to the three branches of the legislature, and which is expressed by the current phrase, "omnipotence of Parliament," thus became the acknowledged property of the three branches of the Federal legislature; and the old and respectable doctrine of State Independence is now no more than an archæological relic, a piece of historical antiquarianism. Yet the actual attributions of the State authorities cover by far the largest part of the province of Government; and by this division of labour and authority, the problem of fixing for the nation a political centre of gravity is divested of a large part of its difficulty and danger, in some proportions to the limitations of the working precinct.

21. Within that precinct, the initiation as well as the final sanction in the great business of finance is made over to the popular branch of the Legislature, and a most interesting question arises upon the comparative merits of this arrangement, and of our own method, which theoretically throws upon the Crown the responsibility of initiating public charge, and under which, until a recent period, our practise was in actual and even close correspondence with this theory.

22. We next come to a difference still more marked. The Federal Executive is born anew of the nation at the end of each four years, and dies at the end. But, during the course of those years, it is independent, in the person both of the President and of his Ministers, alike of the people, of their representatives, and of that remarkable body, the most remarkable of all the inventions of modern politics, the Senate of the United States. In this important matter, whatever be the relative excellences and defects

---

* [This is a proposition of great importance in a disputed subject-matter; and consequently I have not announced it in a dogmatic manner, but as a portion of what we "seem to perceive" in the progress of the American Constitution. It expresses an opinion formed by me upon an examination of the original documents, and with some attention to the history, which I have always considered, and have often recommended to others, as one of the most fruitful studies of modern politics. This is not the proper occasion to develop its grounds : but I may say that I am not at all disposed to sur_ render it in deference to one or two rather contemptuous critics.—W. E. G., December 1868.]

of the British and American systems, it is most certain that nothing would induce the people of this country, or even the Tory
portion of them, to exchange our own for theirs. It may, indeed,
not be obvious to the foreign eye what is the exact difference of
the two. Both the representative chambers hold the power of the
purse. But in America its conditions are such that it does not
operate in any way on behalf of the Chamber or of the nation, as
against the Executive. In England, on the contrary, its efficiency
has been such that it has worked out for itself channels of effective operation, such as to dispense with its direct use, and avoid
the inconveniences which might be attendant upon that use. A
vote of the House of Commons, declaring a withdrawal of its
confidence, has always sufficed for the purpose of displacing a
Ministry ; nay, persistent obstruction of its measures, and even
lighter causes, have conveyed the hint, which has been obediently
taken. But the people, how is it with them? Do not the people
in England part with their power, and make it over to the House
of Commons, as completely as the American people part with it
to the President? They give it over for four years : we for a
period which on the average is somewhat more : they, to resume it
at a fixed time ; we, on an unfixed contingency, and at a time
which will finally be determined, not according to the popular will,
but according to the views which a Ministry may entertain of its
duty or convenience.

23. All this is true ; but it is not the whole truth. In the
United Kingdom, the people as such cannot commonly act upon
the Ministry as such. But mediately, though not immediately,
they gain the end : for they can work upon that which works upon
the Ministry, namely, on the House of Commons. Firstly, they
have not renounced, like the American people, the exercise of
their power for a given time ; and they are at all times free by
speech, petition, public meeting, to endeavour to get it back in
full by bringing about a dissolution. Secondly, in a Parliament
with nearly 660 members, vacancies occur with tolerable frequency ;
and, as they are commonly filled up forthwith, they continually
modify the colour of the Parliament, conformably, not to the past,
but to the present feeling of the nation ; or, at least, of the constituency, which for practical purposes is different indeed, yet not
very different. But, besides exercising a limited positive influence on the present, they supply a much less limited indication of

the future. Of the members who at a given time sit in the House
of Commons, the vast majority, probably more than nine-tenths,
have the desire to sit there again, after a dissolution which may
come at any moment. They, therefore, study political weather-
wisdom, and in varying degrees adapt themselves to the indications of the sky. It will now be readily perceived how the
popular sentiment in England. so far as it is awake. is not meanly
provided with the ways of making itself respected, whether for the
purpose of displacing and replacing a Ministry, or of constraining
it (as sometimes happens), to alter or reverse its policy sufficiently, at least, to conjure down the gathering and muttering storm.

24. It is true, indeed, that every nation is of necessity, to a
great extent, in the condition of the sluggard with regard to public
policy ; hard to rouse, harder to keep aroused, sure after a little
while to sink back into his slumber :—

"Pressitque jacentem,
Dulcis et alta quies, placidæque simillima morti."—Æn. vi. 522.

The people have a vast, but an encumbered power ; and, in
their struggles with overweening authority, or with property, the
excess of force, which they undoubtedly possess, is more than
counterbalanced by the constant wakefulness of the adversary, by
his knowledge of their weakness, and by his command of opportunity. But this is a fault lying rather in the conditions of human
life than in political institutions. There is no known mode of
making attention and inattention equal in their results. It is
enough to say that in England. when the nation can attend, it can
prevail. So we may say, then, that in the American Union the
Federal Executive is independent for each four years both of the
Congress and of the people. But the British Ministry is largely
dependent on the people whenever the people firmly will it ; and is
always dependent on the House of Commons, except of course
when it can safely and effectually appeal to the people.

25. So far, so good. But if we wish really to understand the
manner in which the Queen's Government over the British Empire
is carried on, we must now prepare to examine into some sharper
contrasts than any which our path has yet brought into view. The
power of the American Executive resides in the person of the
actual President, and passes from him to his successor. His Ministers, grouped around him, are the servants, not only of his
office, but of his mind. The intelligence, which carries on the

Government, has its main seat in him. The responsibility of
failures is understood to fall on him ; and it is round his head that
success sheds its halo. The American Government is described.
truly as a Government composed of three members, of three
powers distinct from one another. The English Government is
likewise so described, not truly, but conventionally. For in the
English Government there has gradually formed itself a fourth
power, entering into and sharing the vitality of each of the other
three, and charged with the business of holding them in harmony
as they march.

26. This Fourth Power is the Ministry, or more properly the
Cabinet. For the rest of the Ministry is subordinate and
ancillary ; and, though it largely shares in many departments the
labours of the Cabinet, yet it has only a secondary and derivative
share in the higher responsibilities. No account of the present
British Constitution is worth having which does not take this
Fourth Power largely and carefully into view. And yet it is not a
distinct power, made up of elements unknown to the other three ;
any more than a sphere contains elements other than those refer-
able to the three co-ordinates, which determine the position of
every point in space. The Fourth Power is parasitical to the
three others ; and lives upon their life, without any separate
existence. One portion of it forms a part, which may be termed
an integral part, of the House of Lords, another of the House of
Commons ; and the two conjointly, nestling within the precinct of
Royalty, form the inner Council of the Crown, assuming the whole
of its responsibilities, and in consequence wielding, as a rule, its
powers. The Cabinet is the three-fold hinge that connects
together for action the British Constitution of King or Queen,
Lords, and Commons. Upon it is concentrated the whole strain
of the Government, and it constitutes from day to day the true
centre of gravity for the working system of the State, although
the ultimate superiority of force resides in the representative
chamber.

27. There is no statute or legal usage of this country which
requires that the Ministers of the Crown should hold seats in the
one or the other House of Parliament. It is perhaps upon this
account that, while most of my countrymen would, as I suppose,
declare it to be a becoming and convenient custom, yet compara-
tively few are aware how near the seat of life the observance lies,

how closely it is connected with the equipoise and unity of the social forces. It is rarely departed from, even in an individual case; never, as far as my knowledge goes, on a wider scale. From accidental circumstances it happened that I was a Secretary of State between December 1845 and July 1846, without a seat in the House of Commons. This (which did not pass wholly without challenge) is, I believe, by much the most notable instance for the last fifty years; and it is only within the last fifty years that our Constitutional system has completely settled down. Before the reform of Parliament, it was always easy to find a place for a Minister excluded from his seat; as Sir Robert Peel, for example, ejected from Oxford University, at once found refuge and repose at Tamworth. I desire to fix attention on the identification, in this country, of the Minister with the member of a House of Parliament.

28. It is, as to the House of Commons especially, an inseparable and vital part of our system. The association of the Ministers with the Parliament, and through the House of Commons with the people, is the counterpart of their association as Ministers with the Crown and the prerogative. The decisions that they take are taken under the competing pressure of a bias this way and a bias that way, and strictly represent what is termed in mechanics the composition of forces. Upon them, thus placed, it devolves to provide that the Houses of Parliament shall loyally counsel and serve the Crown, and that the crown shall act strictly in accordance with its obligations to the nation. I will not presume to say whether the adoption of the rule in America would or would not lay the foundation of a great change in the Federal Constitution; but I am quite sure that the abrogation of it in England would either alter the form of government, or bring about a crisis. That it conduces to the personal comfort of Ministers, I will not undertake to say. The various currents of political and social influences meet edgeways in their persons, much like the conflicting tides in St. George's Channel or the Straits of Dover; for, while they are the ultimate regulators of the relations between the Crown on the one side, and the people through the Houses of Parliament on the other, they have no authority vested in them to coerce or censure either way. Their attitude towards the Houses must always be that of deference; their language that of respect, if not submission. Still more must

their attitude and language towards the Sovereign be the same in
principle, and yet more marked in form; and this, though upon
them lies the ultimate responsibility of deciding what shall be
done in the Crown's name in every branch of administration, and
every department of policy, coupled only with the alternative of
ceasing to be Ministers, if what they may advisedly deem the
requisite power of action be denied them.

29. In the ordinary administration of the government, the
Sovereign personally is, so to speak, behind the scenes; perform-
ing, indeed, many personal acts by the Sign-manual, or otherwise,
but, in each and all of them, covered by the counter-signature or
advice of Ministers, who stand between the august Personage and
the people. There is, accordingly, no more power, under the
form of our Constitution, to assail the Monarch in his personal
capacity, or to assail through him, the line of succession to the
Crown, than there is at chess to put the king in check. In truth,
a good deal, though by no means the whole, of the philosophy of
the British Constitution is represented in this central point of the
wonderful game, against which the only reproach—the reproach of
Lord Bacon—is that it is hardly a relaxation, but rather a serious
tax upon the brain.

30. The Sovereign in England is the symbol of the nation's
unity, and the apex of the social structure; the maker (with
advice) of the laws; the supreme governor of the Church; the
fountain of justice; the sole source of honor; the person to
whom all military, all naval, all civil service is rendered. The
Sovereign owns very large properties; receives and holds, in law,
the entire revenue of the State; appoints and dismisses Ministers; makes treaties; pardons crime, or abates its punishment;
wages war, or concludes peace; summons and dissolves the Parliament; exercises these vast powers for the most part without
any specified restraint of law; and yet enjoys, in regard to these
and every other function, an absolute immunity from consequences.
There is no provision in the law of the United Empire, or in the
machinery of the Constitution, for calling the Sovereign to
account; and only in one solitary and improbable, but perfectly
defined case—that of his submitting to the jurisdiction of the Pope
—is he deprived by Statute of the Throne. Setting aside that
peculiar exception, the offspring of a necessity still freshly felt
when it was made, the Constitution might seem to be founded on

the belief of a real infallibility in its head. Less, at any rate, cannot be said than this. Regal right has, since the revolution of 1688, been expressly founded upon contract; and the breach of that contract destroys the title to the allegiance of the subject. But no provision, other than the general rule of hereditary succession, is made to meet either this case, or any other form of political miscarriage or misdeed. It seems as though the Genius of the Nation would not stain its lips by so much as the mere utterance of such a word ; nor can we put this state of facts into language more justly than by saying that the Constitution would regard the default of the Monarch, with his heirs, as the chaos of the State, and would simply trust to the inherent energies of the several orders of society for its legal reconstruction.

31. The original authorship of the representative system is commonly accorded to the English race. More clear and indisputable is its title to the great political discovery of Constitutional Kingship. And a very great discovery it is. Whether it is destined, in any future day, to minister in its integrity to the needs of the New World, it may be hard to say. In that important branch of its utility which is negative, it completely serves the purposes of the many strong and rising colonies of Great Britain, and saves them all the perplexities and perils attendant upon successions to the headship of the Executive. It presents to them, as it does to us, the symbol of unity, and the object of all our political veneration, which we love to find rather in a person, than in an abstract entity, like the State. But the Old World, at any rate, still is, and may long continue, to constitute the living centre of civilization, and to hold the primacy of the race ; and of this great society the several members approximate, in a rapidly extending series, to the practice and idea of Constitutional Kingship. The chief States of Christendom, with only two exceptions, have, with more or less distinctness, adopted it. Many of them, both great and small, have thoroughly assimilated it to their system. The autocracy of Russia, and the Republic of France, each of them congenial to the present wants of the respective countries, may yet, hereafter, gravitate towards the principle, which elsewhere has developed so large an attractive power. Should the current, that has prevailed through the last half-century, maintain its direction and its strength, another fifty years may see all Europe adhering to the theory and practice of this

beneficent institution, and peaceably sailing in the wake of England.

32. No doubt, if tried by an ideal standard, it is open to criticism. Aristotle and Plato, nay, Bacon, and perhaps Leibnitz, would have scouted it as a scientific abortion. Some men would draw disparaging comparisons between the mediæval and the modern King. In the person of the first was normally embodied the force paramount over all others in the country, and on him was laid a weight of responsibility and toil so tremendous, that his function seems always to border upon the superhuman; that his life commonly wore out before the natural term; and that an indescribable majesty, dignity, and interest surround him in his misfortunes, nay, almost in his degradation; as, for instance, amidst

> "The shrieks of death, through Berkeley's roof that ring,
> Shrieks of an agonising King." *

33. For this concentration of power, toil, and liability, milder realities have now been substituted; and Ministerial responsibility comes between the Monarch and every public trial and necessity, like armour between the flesh and the spear that would seek to pierce it; only this is an armour itself also fleshy, at once living and impregnable. It may be said, by an adverse critic, that the Constitutional Monarch is only a depositary of power, as an armoury is a depository of arms; but that those who wield the arms, and those alone, constitute the true governing authority. And no doubt this is so far true, that the scheme aims at associating in the work of government with the head of the State the persons best adapted to meet the wants and wishes of the people, under the conditions that the several aspects of supreme power shall be severally allotted; dignity and visible authority shall lie wholly with the wearer of the crown, but labour mainly, and responsibility wholly with its servants. From hence, without doubt, it follows that should differences arise, it is the will of those in whose minds the work of government is elaborated that in the last resort must prevail. From mere labour, power may be severed; but not from labour joined with responsibility. This capital and vital consequence flows out of the principle that the political action of the Monarch shall everywhere be mediate and conditional upon the concurrence of confidential advisers. It is

---

* Gray's 'Bard.'

impossible to reconcile any, even the smallest, abatement of this doctrine, with the perfect, absolute immunity of the Sovereign from consequences. There can be in England no disloyalty more gross, as to its effects, than the superstition which affects to assign to the Sovereign a separate, and, so far as separate, transcendental sphere of political action. Anonymous servility has, indeed, in these last days, hinted such a doctrine ;* but it is no more practicable to make it thrive in England, than to rear the jungles of Bengal on Salisbury Plain.

34. There is, indeed, one great and critical act, the responsibility for which falls momentarily or provisionally on the Sovereign ; it is the dismissal of an existing Ministry, and the appointment of a new one. This act is usually performed with the aid drawn from authentic manifestations of public opinion, mostly such as are obtained through the votes or conduct of the House of Commons. Since the reign of George III there has been but one change of Ministry in which the Monarch acted without the support of these indications. It was when William IV, in 1834, dismissed the Government of Lord Melbourne, which was known to be supported, though after a lukewarm fashion, by a large majority of the existing House of Commons. But the Royal responsibility was, according to the doctrine of our Constitution, completely taken over, *ex post facto*, by Sir Robert Peel, as the person who consented, on the call of the King, to take Lord Melbourne's office. Thus, though the act was rash, and hard to justify, the doctrine of personal immunity was in no way endangered. And here we may notice, that in theory an absolute personal immunity implies a correlative limitation of power. greater than is always found in practice. It can hardly be said that the King's initiative left to Sir R. Peel a freedom perfectly unimpaired. And, most certainly, it was a very real exercise of personal power. The power did not suffice for its end, which was to overset the Liberal predominance ; but it very nearly sufficed. Unconditionally entitled to dismiss the Ministers, the Sovereign can, of course, choose his own opportunity. He may defy the Parliament, if he can count upon the people. William IV, in the year 1834, had neither Parliament nor people with him. His act was within the limits of the Constitution, for it was covered by the responsibility of the acceding Ministry. But it reduced the Liberal

---

* *Quarterly Review*, April, 1878. Art. I.

majority from a number considerably beyond three hundred to
about thirty ; and it constituted an exceptional, but very real and
large action on the politics of the country, by the direct will of
the King. I speak of the immediate effects. Its eventual result
may have been different, for it converted a large disjointed mass
into a smaller but organised and sufficient force, which held the
fortress of power for the six years 1835-41. On this view it may
be said that, if the Royal intervention anticipated and averted
decay from natural causes, then with all its immediate success, it
defeated its own real aim.

35. But this power of dismissing a Ministry at will, large as it
may be under given circumstances, is neither the safest, nor the
only power which, in the ordinary course of things, falls Constitutionally to the personal share of the wearer of the crown. He is
entitled on all subjects coming before the Ministry, to knowledge
and opportunities of discussion, unlimited save by the iron neces-
sities of business. Though decisions must ultimately conform to
the sense of those who are to be responsible for them, yet their
business is to inform and persuade the Sovereign, not to overrule
him. Were it possible for him, within the limits of human time
and strength, to enter actively into all public transactions, he
would be fully entitled to do so. What is actually submitted is
supposed to be the most fruitful and important part, the cream of
affairs. In the discussion of them, the Monarch has more than
one advantage over his advisers. He is permanent, they are
fugitive ; he speaks from the vantage-ground of a station unap-
proachably higher ; he takes a calm and leisurely survey, while
they are worried with the preparatory stages, and their force is
often impaired by the pressure of countless detail. He may be,
therefore, a weighty factor in all deliberations of State. Every
discovery of a blot, that the studies of the Sovereign in the
domain of business enable him to make, strengthens his hands and
enhances his authority. It is plain, then, that there is abundant
scope for mental activity to be at work under the gorgeous robes
of Royalty.

36. This power spontaneously takes the form of influence ;
and the amount of it depends on a variety of circumstances ; on
talent, experience, tact, weight of character, steady, untiring industry, and habitual presence at the seat of government. In proportion as any of these might fail, the real and legitimate influence

of the Monarch over the course of affairs would diminish ; in proportion as they attain to fuller action, it would increase. It is a
moral, not a coercive, influence. It operates through the will and
reason of the Ministry, not over or against them. It would be an
evil and a perilous day for the Monarchy, were any prospective
possessor of the Crown to assume or claim for himself final, or
preponderating, or even independent power, in any one department
of the State. The ideas and practice of the time of George III,
whose will in certain matters limited the action of the Ministers,
cannot be revived, otherwise than by what would be, on their part,
nothing less than a base compliance, a shameful subserviency, dangerous to the public weal, and, in the highest degree, disloyal to
the dynasty. Because, in every free State, for every public act,
some one must be responsible ; and the question is, Who shall it
be? The British Constitution answers : The Minister, and the
Minister exclusively. That he may be responsible, all action
must be fully shared by him. Sole action, for the Sovereign,
would mean undefended, unprotected action ; the armour of irre-
sponsibility would not cover the whole body against sword or spear ;
a head would project beyond the awning, and would invite a sun-
stroke.

37. The reader, then, will clearly see that there is no distinction more vital to the practice of the British Constitution, or to a
right judgment upon it, than the distinction between the Sovereign
and the Crown. The Crown has large prerogatives, endless functions essential to the daily action, and even the life of the State.
To place them in the hands of persons who should be mere tools
in a Royal will, would expose those powers to constant unsup-
ported collision with the living forces of the nation, and to a
certain and irremediable crash. They are therefore entrusted to
men, who must be prepared to answer for the use they make of
them. This ring of responsible Ministerial agency forms a fence
around the person of the Sovereign, which has thus far proved
impregnable to all assaults. The august personage, who from
time to time may rest within it, and who may possess the art of
turning to the best account the countless resources of the position,
is no dumb and senseless idol ; but, together with real and very
large means of influence upon policy, enjoys the undivided reverence which a great people feels for its head ; and is likewise the
first and ,by far the weightiest among the forces, which greatly
mould, by example and legitimate authority, the manners, nay the

morals, of a powerful aristocracy and a wealthy and highly trained society. The social influence of a Sovereign, even if it stood alone, would be an enormous attribute. The English people are not believers in equality; they do not, with the famous Declaration of July 4th, 1776, think it to be a self-evident truth that all men are born equal. They hold rather the reverse of that proposition. At any rate, in practice, they are what I may call determined inequalitarians; nay, in some cases, even without knowing it. Their natural tendency, from the very base of British society, and through all its strongly built gradations, is to look upwards: they are not apt to "untune degree." The Sovereign is the highest height of the system; is, in that system, like Jupiter among the Roman gods, first without a second.

"Nec viget quicquam simile aut secundum."*

Not like Mont Blanc, with rivals in his neighbourhood; but like Ararat or Etna, towering alone and unapproachable. The step downward from the King to the second person in the realm is not like that from the second to the third: it is more even than a stride, for it traverses a gulf. It is the wisdom of the British Constitution to lodge the personality of its chief so high, that none shall under any circumstances be tempted to vie, no, nor dream of vieing, with it. The office, however, is not confused, though it is associated, with the person; and the elevation of official dignity in the Monarch of these realms has now for a testing period worked well, in conjunction with the limitation of merely personal power.

38. In the face of the country, the Sovereign and the Ministers are an absolute unity. The one may concede to the other; but the limit of concessions by the Sovereign is at the point where he becomes willing to try the experiment of changing his Government; and the limit of concession by the Ministers is at the point where they become unwilling to bear, what in all circumstances they must bear while they remain Ministers, the undivided responsibility of all that is done in the Crown's name. But it is not with the Sovereign only that the Ministry must be welded into identity. It has a relation to sustain to the House of Lords; which need not, however, be one of entire unity, for the House of Lords, though a great power in the State, and able to cause great embarrassment to an Administration, is not able by a vote to

* Hor. Od. I. xii. 18.

doom it to capital punishment. Only for fifteen years, out of the last fifty, has the Ministry of the day possessed the confidence of the House of Lords. On the confidence of the House of Commons it is immediately and vitally dependent. This confidence it must always possess, either absolutely from identity of political colour, or relatively and conditionally. This last case arises when an accidental dislocation of the majority in the Chamber has put the machine for the moment out of gear, and the unsafe experiment of a sort of provisional government, doomed on the one hand to be feeble, or tempted on the other to be dishonest, is tried; much as the Roman Conclave has sometimes been satisfied with a provisional Pope, deemed likely to live for the time necessary to re-unite the fractions of the prevailing party.

39. I have said that the Cabinet is essentially the regulator of the relations between King, Lords, and Commons; exercising functionally the powers of the first, and incorporated, in the persons of its members, with the second and the third. It is, therefore, itself a great power. But let no one suppose it is the greatest. In a balance nicely poised, a small weight may turn the scale; and the helm that directs the ship is not stronger than the ship. It is a cardinal axiom of the modern British Constitution, that the House of Commons is the greatest of the powers of the State. It might, by a base subserviency, fling itself at the feet of a Monarch or a Minister; it might, in a season of exhaustion, allow the slow persistence of the Lords, ever eyeing it as Lancelot was eyed by Modred, to invade its just province by baffling its action at some time propitious for the purpose. But no Constitution can anywhere keep either Sovereign, or Assembly, or nation, true to its trust and to itself. All that can be done has been done. The Commons are armed with ample powers of self-defence. If they use their powers properly, they can only be mastered by a recurrence to the people, and the way in which the appeal can succeed is by the choice of another House of Commons more agreeable to the national temper. Thus the sole appeal from the verdict of the House is a rightful appeal to those from whom it received its commission.

40. This superiority in power among the great State forces was, in truth, established even before the House of Commons became what it now is, representative of the people throughout its entire area. In the early part of the century, a large part of its members virtually received their mandate from members of the

Peerage, or from the Crown, or by the direct action of money on a
mere handful of individuals, or, as in Scotland for example, from
constituencies whose limited numbers and upper-class sympathies
usually shut out popular influences. A real supremacy belonged
to the House as a whole; but the forces of which it was com-
pounded were not all derived from the people, and the aristocratic
power had found out the secret of asserting itself within the walls
of the popular chamber, in the dress and through the voices of its
members. Many persons of gravity and weight saw great danger
in a measure of change like the first Reform Act, which left it to
the Lords to assert themselves, thereafter, by an external force,
instead of through a share in the internal composition of a body
so formidable. But the result proved that they were sufficiently to
exercise, through the popular will and choice, the power which
they had formerly put in action without its sanction, though
within its proper precinct and with its title falsely inscribed.

41. The House of Commons is superior, and by far superior,
in the force of its political attributes, to any other single power in
the State. But it is watched; it is criticised; it is hemmed in
and about by a multitude of other forces; the force, first of all,
of the House of Lords, the force of opinion from day to day, particularly of the highly anti-popular opinion of the leisured men of
the metropolis, who, seated close to the scene of action, wield an
influence greatly in excess of their just claims; the force of the
classes and professions; the just and useful force of the local
authorities in their various orders and places. Never was the
great problem more securely solved, which recognises the necessity
of a paramount power in the body politic to enable it to move, but
requires for it a depository such that it shall be safe against invasion, and yet inhibited from aggression.

42. The old theories of a mixed government, and of the three
powers, coming down from the age of Cicero, when set by the side
of the living British Constitution, are cold, crude, and insufficient
to a degree that makes them deceptive. Take them, for example,
as represented, fairly enough, by Voltaire : the picture drawn by
him is for us nothing but a puzzle :—

> "Aux murs de Vestminster on voit paraître ensemble
> Trois pouvoirs étonnés du nœud qui les rassemble,
> Les députés du peuple, les grands, et le Roi,
> Divisés d'intérét, réunis par la Loi."*

---

* Henriade, I.

There is here lacking an amalgam, a reconciling power, what may be called a clearing-house of political forces, which shall draw into itself everything, and shall balance and adjust everything, and ascertaining the net result, let it pass on freely for the fulfilment of the purposes of the great social union. Like a stout buffer-spring, it receives all shocks, and within it their opposing elements neutralise one another. This is the function of the British Cabinet. It is perhaps the most curious formation in the political world of modern times, not for its dignity, but for its subtlety. its elasticity, and its many-sided diversity of power. It is the complement of the entire system; a system which appears to want nothing but a thorough loyalty in the persons composing its several parts, with a reasonable intelligence, to insure its bearing, without fatal damage, the wear and tear of ages yet to come.

43. It has taken more than a couple of centuries to bring the British Cabinet to its present accuracy and fulness of development; for the first rudiments of it may sufficiently be discerned in the reign of Charles I. Under Charles II it had fairly started from its embryo ; and the name is found both in Clarendon and in the Diary of Pepys.* It was for a long time without a Ministerial head ; the King was the head. While this arrangement subsisted, Constitutional government could be but half established. Of the numerous titles of the Revolution of 1688 to respect, not the least remarkable is this, that the great families of the country, and great powers of the State, made no effort, as they might have done, in the hour of its weakness, to aggrandise themselves at the expense of the Crown. Nevertheless, for various reasons, and among them because of the foreign origin, and absences from time to time, of several Sovereigns, the course of events tended to give force to the organs of Government actually on the spot, and thus to consolidate, and also to uplift, this as yet novel creation. So late, however, as the impeachment of Sir Robert Walpole, his friends thought it expedient to urge on his behalf, in the House of Lords, that he had never presumed to constitute himself a Prime Minister.

44. The breaking down of the great offices of State by throwing them into commission, and last among them of the Lord High Treasurership after the time of Harley, Earl of Oxford, tended, and may probably have been meant, to prevent or retard the for-

mation of a recognised Chiefship in the Ministry ; which even now we have not learned to designate by a true English word, though the use of the imported phrase "Premier" is at least as old as the poetry of Burns. Nor can anything be more curiously characteristic of the political genius of the people, than the present position of this most important official personage. Departmentally, he is no more than the first named of five persons, by whom jointly the powers of the Lord Treasurership are taken to be exercised ; he is not their master, or, otherwise than by mere priority, their head: and he has no special function or prerogative under the formal constitution of the office. He has no official rank, except that of Privy Councillor. Eight members of the Cabinet, including five Secretaries of State, and several other members of the Government, take official precedence of him. His rights and duties as head of the Administration are nowhere recorded. He is almost, if not altogether, unknown to the Statute Law.

45. Nor is the position of the body, over which he presides, less singular than his own. The Cabinet wields, with partial exceptions, the Powers of the Privy Council, besides having a standing ground in relation to the personal will of the Sovereign, far beyond what the Privy Council ever held or claimed. Yet it has no connection with the Privy Council, except that every one, on first becoming a member of the Cabinet, is, if not belonging to it already, sworn a member of that body. There are other sections of the Privy Council, forming regular Committees for Education and for Trade. But the Cabinet has not even this degree of formal sanction, to sustain its existence. It lives and acts simply by understanding, without a single line of written law or constitution to determine its relations to the Monarch, or to the Parliament, or to the nation ; or the relations of its members to one another, or to their head. It sits in the closest secrecy. There is no record of its proceedings, nor is there any one to hear them, except upon the very rare occasions when some important functionary, for the most part military or legal, is introduced, *pro hac vice*, for the purpose of giving to it necessary information.

46. Every one of its members acts in no less than three capacities : as administrator of a department of State ; as member of a legislative chamber ; and as a confidential adviser of the Crown. Two at least of them add to those three characters a fourth ; for

in each House of Parliament it is indispensable that one of the principal Ministers should be what is termed its Leader. This is an office the most indefinite of all, but not the least important. With very little of defined prerogative, the Leader suggests, and in a great degree fixes, the course of all principal matters of business, supervises and keeps in harmony the action of his colleagues, takes the initiative in matters of ceremonial procedure, and advises the House in every difficulty as it arises. The first of these, which would be of but secondary consequence where the assembly had time enough for all its duties, is of the most utmost weight in our overcharged House of Commons, where, notwithstanding all its energy and all its diligence, for one thing of consequence that is done, five or ten are despairingly postponed. The overweight, again, of the House of Commons is apt, other things being equal, to bring its Leader inconveniently near in power to a Prime Minister who is a Peer. He can play off the House of Commons against his chief; and instances might be cited, though they are happily most rare, when he has served him very ugly tricks.

47. The nicest of all the adjustments involved in the working of the British Government is that which determines, without formally defining, the internal relations of the Cabinet. On the one hand, while each Minister is an adviser of the Crown, the Cabinet is an unity, and none of its members can advise as an individual, without, or in opposition actual or presumed to, his colleagues. On the other hand, the business of the State is a hundredfold too great in volume to allow of the actual passing of the whole under the view of the collected Ministry. It is therefore a prime office of discretion for each Minister to settle what are the departmental acts in which he can presume the concurrence of his colleagues, and in what more delicate, or weighty, or peculiar cases, he must positively ascertain it. So much for the relation of each Minister to the Cabinet; but here we touch the point which involves another relation, perhaps the least known of all, his relation to its head.

48. The head of the British Government is not a Grand Vizier. He has no powers, properly so called, over his colleagues: on the rare occasions, when a Cabinet determines its course by the votes of its members, his vote counts only as one of theirs. But they are appointed and dismissed by the Sovereign on his advice. In a perfectly organised administration, such for example as was that of Sir Robert Peel in 1841-6, nothing of great importance is

matured, or would even be projected, in any department without his
personal cognisance ; and any weighty business would commonly
go to him before being submitted to the Cabinet. He reports to
the Sovereign its proceedings, and he also has many audiences of
the august occupant of the Throne. He is bound, in these reports and audiences, not to counterwork the Cabinet; not to
divide it ; not to undermine the position of any of his colleagues
in the Royal favour. If he departs in any degree from strict ad-
herence to these rules, and uses his great opportunities to increase
his own influence, or pursue aims not shared by his colleagues,
then, unless he is prepared to advise their dismissal, he not only
departs from rule, but commits an act of treachery and baseness.
As the Cabinet stands between the Sovereign and the Parliament,
and is bound to be loyal to both, so he stands between his colleagues and the Sovereign, and is bound to be loyal to both. '

49. As a rule, the resignation of the First Minister, as if removing the bond of cohesion in the Cabinet, has the effect of dis-
solving it. A conspicuous instance of this was furnished by Sir
Robert Peel in 1846 ; when the dissolution of the Administration,
after it had carried the repeal of the Corn Laws, was understood
to be due not so much to a united deliberation and decision as to
his initiative. The resignation of any other Minister only creates
a vacancy. In certain circumstances, the balance of forces may
be so delicate and susceptible that a single resignation will break
up the Government ; but what is the rule in the one case is the
rare exception in the other. The Prime Minister has no title to
override any one of his colleagues in any one of the departments.
So far as he governs them, unless it is done by trick, which is not
to be supposed, he governs them by influence only. But upon the
whole, nowhere in the wide world does so great a substance cast
so small a shadow ; nowhere is there a man who has so much
power, with so little to show for it in the way of formal title or
prerogative.

50. The slight record that has here been traced may convey but
a faint idea of an unique creation. And, slight as it is, I believe
it tells more than, except in the school of British practice, is elsewhere to be learned of a machine so subtly balanced, that it
seems as though it were moved by something not less delicate and
slight than the mainspring of a watch. It has not been the offspring of the thought of man. The Cabinet, and all the present
relations of the Constitutional powers in this country, have grown

into their present dimensions, and settled into their present places, not as the fruit of a philosophy, not in the effort to give effect to an abstract principle ; but by the silent action of forces, invisible and insensible, the structure has come up into the view of all the world. It is, perhaps, the most conspicuous object on the wide political horizon ; but it has thus risen, without noise, like the temple of Jerusalem.

"No workman steel, no ponderous hammers rung;
Like some tall palm the stately fabric sprung."*

51. When men repeat the proverb which teaches us that "marriages are made in heaven," what they mean is that, in the most fundamental of all social operations, the building up of the family, the issues involved in the nuptial contract, lie beyond the best exercise of human thought, and the unseen forces of providential government make good the defect in our imperfect capacity. Even so would it seem to have been in that curious marriage of competing influences and powers, which brings about the composite harmony of the British Constitution. More, it must be admitted, than any other, it leaves open doors which lead into blind alleys ; for it presumes, more boldly than any other, the good sense and good faith of those who work it. If, unhappily, these personages meet together, on the great arena of a nation's fortunes, as jockeys meet upon a racecourse, each to urge to the uttermost, as against the others, the power of the animal he rides, or as counsel in a court, each to procure the victory of his client, without respect to any other interest or right ; then this boasted Constitution of ours is neither more nor less than a heap of absurdities. The undoubted competency of each reaches even to the paralysis or destruction of the rest. The House of Commons is entitled to refuse every shilling of the Supplies. That House, and also the House of Lords, is entitled to refuse its assent to every Bill presented to it. The Crown is entitled to make a thousand Peers to-day and as many to-morrow ; it may dissolve all and every Parliament before it proceeds to business ; may pardon the most atrocious crimes ; may declare war against all the world ; may conclude treaties involving unlimited responsibilities, and even vast expenditure, without the consent, nay without the

---

* Heber's 'Palestine.' The word "stately" was in later editions altered by the author to "noiseless."

knowledge, of Parliament, and this not merely in support or in
development, but in reversal, of policy already known to and
sanctioned by the nation. But the assumption is that the deposi-
taries of power will all respect one another; will evince a con-
sciousness that they are working in a common interest for a
common end; that they will be possessed, together with not less
than an average intelligence, of not less than an average sense of
equity and of the public interest and rights. When these reasonable expectations fail, then, it must be admitted, the British Constitution will be in danger.

52. Apart from such contingencies, the offspring only of folly
or of crime, this Constitution is peculiarly liable to subtle
change. Not only in the long-run, as man changes between
youth and age, but also, like the human body, with a quotidian
life, a periodical recurrence of ebbing and flowing tides. Its old
particles daily run to waste, and give place to new. What is
hoped among us is, that which has usually been found, that evils
will become palpable before they have grown to be intolerable.

53. There cannot, for example, be much doubt among careful
observers that the great conservator of liberty in all former times,
namely, the confinement of the power of the purse to the popular
chamber, has been lamentably weakened in its efficiency of late
years; weakened in the House of Commons, and weakened by the
House of Commons. It might indeed be contended that the House
of Commons of the present epoch does far more to increase the
aggregate of public charge than to reduce it. It might even
be a question whether the public would take benefit if the House
were either entrusted annually with a great part of the initiative,
so as to be really responsible to the people for the spending of
their money; or else were excluded from part at least of its direct
action upon expenditure, entrusting to the executive the application of given sums which that executive should have no legal
power to exceed.

54. Meantime we of this island are not great political
philosophers; and we contend with an earnest, but disproportioned,
vehemence about changes which are palpable, such as the extension of the suffrage, on the redistribution of Parliamentary seats,
neglecting wholly other processes of change which work beneath
the surface, and in the dark, but which are even more fertile of
great organic results. The modern English character reflects the

English Constitution in this, that it abounds in paradox; that it possesses every strength, but holds it tainted with every weakness; that it seems alternately both to rise above and to fall below the standard of average humanity; that there is no allegation of praise or blame which, in some one of the aspects of its many-sided formation, it does not deserve; that only in the midst of much default, and much transgression, the people of this United Kingdom either have heretofore established, or will hereafter establish, their title to be reckoned among the children of men, for the eldest born of an imperial race.

55. In this imperfect survey, I have carefully avoided all reference to the politics of the day and to particular topics, recently opened, which may have undergone a great development even before these lines appear in print on the other side of the Atlantic. Such reference would, without any countervailing advantage, have lowered the strain of these remarks, and would have complicated with painful considerations a statement essentially impartial and general in its scope.

56. For the yet weightier reason of incompetency, I have avoided the topics of chief present interest in America, including that proposal to tamper with the true monetary creed which (as we would say) the Tempter lately presented to the nation in the Silver Bill. But I will not close this paper without recording my conviction that the great acts, and the great forbearances, which immediately followed the close of the Civil War form a group which will ever be a noble object, in his political retrospect, to the impartial historian; and that, proceeding as they did from the free choice and conviction of the people, and founded as they were on the very principles of which the multitude is supposed to be least tolerant, they have, in doing honour to the United States, also rendered a splendid service to the general cause of popular government throughout the world.*

---

* [In reply to the intended work of Mr. Adams on the Constitution of the United States, Mr. Livingstone, under the title of a Colonist of New Jersey, published an Examination of the British Constitution, and compared it unfavourably as it had been exhibited by Adams, and by Delolme, with the institutions of his own country. In this work, of which I have a French translation (London and Paris, 1789), there is not the smallest inkling of the action of our political mechanism, such as I have endeavoured to describe it. On this subject I need hardly refer the reader to the valuable work of Mr. Bagehot, entitled 'The English Constitution,' or to the Constitutional History of Sir T. Erskine May.—W. E. G., December 1878.]

IV

THE GROWTH OF THE ENGLISH CONSTITUTION.

[From E. A. Freeman's "Growth of the English Constitution," Chap. III].

In my two former chapters I have carried my brief sketch of the history of the English Constitution down to the great events of the seventeenth century. I chose that point as the end of my consecutive narrative, because the peculiar characteristic of the times which have followed has been that so many and such important practical changes have been made without any change in the written Law, without any re-enactment of the Law, without any fresh declaration of its meaning. The movements and revolutions of former times, as I have before said, seldom sought any acknowledged change in the Law, but rather its more distinct enactment, its more careful and honest administration. This was the general character of all the great steps in our political history, from the day when William of Normandy renewed the Laws of Eadward, to the day when William of Orange gave his royal assent to the Bill of Rights. But, though each step in our progress took the shape, not of the creation of a new right, but of the firmer establishment of an old one, yet each step was marked by some formal and public act which stands enrolled among the landmarks of our progress. Some Charter was granted by the Sovereign, some Act of Parliament was passed by the Estates of the Realm, setting forth in legal form the nature and measure of the rights which it was sought to place on a firmer ground. Since the seventeenth century things have in this respect greatly altered. The work of legislation, of strictly constitutional legislation, has never ceased; a long succession of legislative enactments stand out as landmarks of political progress no less in more recent than in earlier times. But alongside of them there has also been a series of political changes, changes of no less moment than those which

are recorded in the statute-book, which have been made without
any legislative enactment whatever. A whole code of political
maxims, universally acknowledged in theory, universally carried
out in practice, has grown up, without leaving among the formal
acts of our legislature any trace of the steps by which it
grew. Up to the end of the seventeenth century, we may fairly
say that no distinction could be drawn between the Constitution and the Law. The prerogative of the Crown, the privilege
of Parliament, the liberty of the subject, might not always be
clearly defined on every point. It has indeed been said that those
three things were all of them things to which in their own nature no limit could be set. But all three were supposed to rest,
if not on the direct words of the Statute Law, yet at least on
that somewhat shadowy yet very practical creation, that mixture
of genuine ancient traditions and of recent devices of lawyers,
which is known to Englishmen as the Common Law. Any breach
either of the rights of the Sovereign or of the rights of the
subject was a legal offence, capable of legal definition and sub-
jecting the offender to legal penalties. An act which could
not be brought within the letter either of the Statute or of the
Common Law would not then have been looked upon as an offence
at all. If lower courts were too weak to do justice, the High
Court of Parliament stood ready to do justice even against the
mightiest offenders. It was armed with weapons fearful and
rarely used, but none the less regular and legal. It could smite
by impeachment, by attainder, by the exercise of the greatest
power of all, the deposition of the reigning King. But men had
not yet reached the more subtle doctrine that there may be offences
against the Constitution which are no offences against the Law.
They had not learned that men in high office may have a responsibility practically felt and acted on, but which no legal enactment
has defined, and which no legal tribunal can enforce. It had not
been found out that Parliament itself has a power, now practically
the highest of its powers, in which it acts neither as a legislature
nor as a court of justice, but in which it pronounces sentences
which have none the less practical force because they carry with
them none of the legal consequences of death, bonds, banishment,
or confiscation. We now have a whole system of political moral-
ity, a whole code of precepts for the guidance of public men,
which will not be found in any page of either the Statute or the

Common Law, but which are in practice held hardly less sacred than any principle embodied in the Great Charter or in the Petition of Right. In short, by the side of our written Law, there has grown up an unwritten or conventional Constitution. When an Englishman speaks of the conduct of a public man being constitutional or unconstitutional, he means something wholly different from what he means by conduct being legal or illegal. A famous vote of the House of Commons, passed on the motion of a great statesman, once declared that the then Ministers of the Crown did not possess the confidence of the House of Commons, and that their continuance in office was therefore at variance with the spirit of the Constitution. The truth of such a position, according to the traditional principles on which public men have acted for some generations, cannot be disputed ; but it would be in vain to seek for any trace of such doctrines in any page of our written Law. The proposer of that motion did not mean to charge the existing Ministry with any illegal act, with any act which could be made the subject either of a prosecution in a lower court or of impeachment in the High Court of Parliament itself. He did not mean that they, Ministers of the Crown, appointed during the pleasure of the Crown, committed any breach of the Law of which the Law could take cognizance, by retaining possession of their offices till such time as the Crown should think good to dismiss them from those offices. What he meant was that the general course of their policy was one which to a majority of the House of Commons did not seem to be wise or beneficial to the nation, and that therefore, according to a conventional code as well understood and as effectual as the written Law itself, they were bound to resign offices of which the House of Commons no longer held them to be worthy. The House made no claim to dismiss those Ministers from their offices by any act of its own ; it did not even petition the Crown to remove them from their offices. It simply spoke its mind on their general conduct, and it was held that, when the House had so spoken, it was their duty to give way without any formal petition, without any formal command, on the part either of the House or of the Sovereign. The passing by the House of Commons of such a resolution as this may perhaps be set down as the formal declaration of a constitutional principle. But though a formal declaration, it was not a legal declaration. It created a precedent for the practical guidance of future Ministers and future Parliaments, but it neither changed the Law nor declared it. It asserted a principle which might be appealed to in future debates in the House of Commons, but it asserted no principle which could be taken any notice of by a Judge in any Court of Law. It stands therefore on a wholly different ground from those enactments which, whether they changed the Law or simply declared the Law, had a real legal force, capable of being enforced by a legal tribunal. If any officer of the Crown should levy a tax without the authority of Parliament, if he should enforce martial law without the authority of Parliament, he would be guilty of a legal crime. But, if he merely continues to hold an office conferred by the Crown and from which the Crown has not removed him, though he hold in teeth of any number of votes of censure passed by both Houses of Parliament, he is in no way a breaker of the written Law. But the man who should so act would be universally held to have trampled under foot one of the most undoubted principles of the unwritten but universally accepted Constitution.

The remarkable thing is that, of these two kinds of hypothetical offences, the latter, whose guilt is purely conventional, is almost as unlikely to happen as the former, whose guilt is a matter established by Law. The power of the Law is so firmly established among us that the possibility of breaches of the Law on the part of the Crown or its Ministers hardly ever comes into our heads. And conduct sinning against the broad lines of the unwritten Constitution is looked on as almost as unlikely. Political men may debate whether such and such a course is or is not constitutional, just as lawyers may debate whether such a course is or is not legal. But the very form of the debate implies that there is a Constitution to be observed, just as in the other case it implies that there is a Law to be observed. Now this firm establishment of a purely unwritten and conventional code is one of the most remarkable facts in history. It is plain that it implies the firmest possible establishment of the power of the written Law as its groundwork. If there were the least fear of breaches of the written Law on the part of the Crown or its officers, we should be engaged in finding means to getting rid of that more serious danger, not in disputing over points arising out of a code which has no legal existence. But it is well sometimes to stop and remember how thoroughly conventional the whole of our received system is. The received doctrine as to the relations of the two Houses of Parliament to one another, the whole theory of the position of the body known as the Cabinet and of its chief the Prime Minister, every detail in short of the practical working of government among us, is a matter belonging wholly to the unwritten Constitution and not at all to the written Law. The limits of the royal authority are indeed clearly defined by the written Law. But I suspect that many people would be amazed at the amount of power which the Crown still possesses by Law, and at the many things, which in our eyes would seem utterly monstrous, but which might yet be done by royal authority without any law being broken. The law indeed secures us against arbitrary legislation, against the repeal of any old laws, or the enactment of any new ones, without the consent of both Houses of Parliament. But it is the unwritten Constitution alone which makes it practically impossible for the Crown to refuse its assent to measures which have passed both Houses of Parliament, and which in many cases makes it almost equally impossible to refuse the prayer of an address sent up by one of those Houses only. The written Law leaves to the Crown the choice of all its ministers and agents, great and small; their appointment to office and their removal from office, as long as they commit no crime which the law can punish, is a matter left to the personal discretion of the Sovereign. The unwritten Constitution makes it practically impossible for the Sovereign to keep a Minister in office whom the House of Commons does not approve, and it makes it almost equally impossible to remove from office a Minister whom the House of Commons does approve. The written Law and the unwritten Constitution alike exempt the Sovereign from all ordinary personal responsibility. They both transfer the responsibility from the Sovereign himself to his agents and advisers. But the nature and extent of their responsibility is widely different in the eyes of the written Law and in the eyes of the unwritten Constitution. The written Law is satisfied with holding that the command of the Sovereign is no excuse for an illegal act, and that he who advises the commission of an illegal act by royal authority must bear the responsibility from which the Sovereign himself is free. The written Law knows nothing of any responsibility but such as may be enforced either by prosecution in any of the ordinary Courts or by impeachment in the High Court of Parliament. The unwritten Constitution subjects the agents and advisers of the Crown to a responsibility of quite another kind. What we understand by the responsibility of Ministers is that they are liable to have all their public acts discussed in Parliament, not only on the ground of their legal or illegal character, but on the vaguest grounds of their general tendency. They may be in no danger of prosecution or impeachment; but they are no less bound to bow to other indications of the will of the House of Commons; the unwritten Constitution makes a vote of censure as effectual as an impeachment, and in many cases it makes a mere refusal to pass a ministerial measure as effectual as a vote of censure. The written Law knows nothing of the Cabinet or the Prime Minister; it knows them as members of one or the other House of Parliament, as Privy Councillors, as holders each man in his own person of certain offices, but, as a collective body bound together by a common responsibility, the Law never heard of them. But in the eye of the unwritten Constitution the Prime Minister and the Cabinet of which he is the head form the main feature of our system of government. It is plain at a moment's glance that the practical power of the Crown is not now what it was in the reign of William the Third or even in that of George the Third. But the change is due, far less to changes in the written Law than to changes in the unwritten Constitution. The Law leaves the powers of the Crown untouched, but the Constitution requires that those powers should be exercised by such persons, and in such a manner, as may be acceptable to a majority of the House of Commons. In all these ways, in a manner silent and indirect, the Lower House of Parliament, as it is still deemed in formal rank, has become the really ruling power in the nation. There is no greater contrast than that which exists between the humility of its formal dealings with the Crown, and even with the Upper House, and the reality of the irresistible power which it exercises over both. It is so conscious of the mighty force of its indirect powers that it no longer cares to claim the direct powers which it exercised in former times. There was a time when Parliament was directly consulted on questions of War and Peace. There was a time when Parliament claimed directly to appoint several of the chief officers of State. There were much later times when it was no unusual thing to declare a man in power to be a public enemy, or directly to address the Crown for his removal from office and from the royal presence. No such direct exercises of parliamentary power are needed now, because the whole machinery of government may be changed by the simple process of the House refusing to pass a measure on which the Minister has made up his mind to stake his official being.

Into the history of the stages by which this most remarkable state of things has been brought about I do not intend here to enter. The code of our unwritten Constitution has, like all other English things, grown up bit by bit, and, for the most part, silently and without any acknowledged author. Yet some stages of the development are easily pointed out, and they make important landmarks. The beginning may be placed in the reign of William the Third, when we first find anything at all like a *Ministry* in the modern sense. Up to that time the servants of the Crown had been servants of the Crown, each man in the personal discharge of his own office. The holder of each office owed faithful service to the Crown, and he was withal responsible to the Law; but he stood in no special fellowship towards the holder of any other office. Provided he discharged his own duties, nothing hindered him from being the personal or political enemy of any of his fellow-servants. It was William who first saw that, if the King's government was to be carried on, there must be at least a general agreement of opinions and aims among the King's chief agents in his government. From this beginning a system has gradually grown up which binds the chief officers of the Crown to work together in at least outward harmony, to undertake the defence of one another, and on vital points to stand and fall together. Another important stage happened in much later times, when the King ceased to take a share in person in the deliberations of his Cabinet. And I may mark a change in language which has happened within my own memory, and which, like other changes of language, is certainly not without its meaning. We now familiarly speak, in Parliament and out of Parliament, of the body of Ministers actually in power, the body known to the Constitution but wholly unknown to the Law, by the name of "the Government." We speak of "Mr. Gladstone's Government" or "Mr. Disraeli's Government." I can myself remember the time when such a form of words was unknown, when "Government" still meant "Government by King, Lords, and Commons," and when the body of men who acted as th? King's immediate advisers were spoken of as "Ministers" or "the Ministry."

This kind of silent, I might say stealthy, growth, has, without the help of any legislative enactment, produced that unwritten and conventional code of political rules which we speak of as the Constitution. This process I have spoken of as being character-istic of the days since the Revolution of 1688, as distinguished from earlier times. And so it undoubtedly is. At no earlier time have so many important changes in constitutional doctrine and practice won universal acceptance without being recorded in any written enactment. Yet this tendency of later times is, after all, only a further development of a tendency which was at work from the beginning. It is simply another application of the Eng-lishman's love of precedent. The growth of the unwritten Con-stitution has much in common with the earlier growth of the unwritten Common Law. I have shown in earlier chapters that some of the most important principles of our earlier Constitution were established silently and by the power of precedent, without resting on any known written enactment. If we cannot show any Act of Parliament determining the relations in which the members of the Cabinet stand to the Crown, to the House of Commons, and to one another, neither can we show the Act of Parliament which decreed, in opposition to the practice of all other nations, that the children of the hereditary Peer should be simple Commoners. The real difference is that, in more settled times, when Law was fully supreme, it was found that many im-portant practical changes might be made without formal changes in the Law. It was also found that there is a large class of political subjects which can be better dealt with in this way of tacit understandings than they can be in the shape of a formal enact-ment by Law. We practically understand what is meant by Ministers having or not having the confidence of the House of Commons ; we practically recognize the cases in which, as not having the confidence of the House, they ought to resign office and the cases in which they may fairly appeal to the country by a dissolution of Parliament. But it would be utterly impossible to define such cases beforehand in the terms of an Act of Parliament. Or again, the Speaker of the House of Commons is an officer known to the Law. The Leader of the House of Commons is a person as well known to the House and the country, his functions are well understood, as those of the Speaker himself. But of the Leader of the House of Commons the Law knows nothing. It would be hopeless to seek to define his duties in any legal form, and the House itself has, before now, shrunk from recognizing the existence of such a person in any shape of which a Court of Law could take notice.

During a time then which is now not very far short of two hundred years, the silent and extra-legal growth of our conventional Constitution has been at least as important as the actual changes in our written Law.

V.

STAGES IN THE DEVELOPMENT OF THE CABINET.

[From "Central Government." By H. D. Traill, in the "English Citizen Series."]

It remains to glance briefly at the steps by which the Cabinet, after it once became recognised as the supreme consultative body, developed the precise character, attributes and mutual relations of parts, which at present distinguish it.

It has been said that the first step towards establishing its effective parliamentary responsibility was the introduction of the King's ministers into Parliament. But it must not be supposed that the advantage of this change was immediately recognized by those to whom this advantage accrued. On the contrary, the policy of William III in this respect was at first regarded with jealousy. The House of Commons of that day, which had already grown impatient of the number of minor dependents upon the Crown who had found their way into its ranks, made several legislative attempts to exclude all office-holders from a seat; and finally succeeded in procuring their prospective exclusion by introducing a clause into an Act of 1700, whereby it was provided .that, on the accession of the House of Hanover, no person who had an office or place of profit under the King, or received a pension from the Crown, should be capable of serving as a member of the House of Commons. But the event in contemplation did not take place till fourteen years after, and before half that period had elapsed the advantages of the presence of Cabinet Ministers in the Legislature had become so manifest that Parliament repealed the exclusory clause of its former enactment, and substituted for it the wiser provision that members accepting offices of profit from the Crown should simply vacate their seats, but should (with certain exceptions not necessary to specify here) be capable of re-election by their constituents.

From this time forth, then, we find the same relations established between Cabinet and Parliament which prevail in our own day. But the relations of the members of the Cabinet among themselves were at first very different from what now exist, and a good many years were destined to pass before things finally settled down into their present position. There are three principal points in which this process is to be traced.

1. *Political Unanimity.*—It would seem very strange to us in these days to see politicians of opposite parties sitting in the same Cabinet; yet that practice was, for many years after the establishment of constitutional government, the rule rather than the exception. The precedent created by William III in the selection of the first party-ministry was, as we have seen, very soon departed from, and was thereafter continually set at nought. The later ministries of the same King were of a mixed character; the ministries of Anne were partly Whig and partly Tory; and the political unity which prevailed in the Walpole administration was succeeded by a return to the old practice under Pulteney. It was not till later that it became an admitted political axiom that Cabinets should be constructed upon some basis of political union, agreed upon by the members composing the same when they accept office together.

2. *Unity of Responsibility.*—As a consequence of the earlier practice of constructing Cabinets of men of different political views, it followed that the members of such Cabinets did not and could not regard their responsibility to Parliament as one and indivisible. The resignation of an important member, of even of the Prime Minister, was not regarded as necessitating the simultaneous retirement of his colleagues. Even as late as the fall of Sir Robert Walpole, fifty years after the Revolution Settlement (and itself the first instance of resignation in deference to a hostile parliamentary vote), we find the King requesting Walpole's successor, Pulteney, "not to distress the Government by making too many changes in the midst of a session"; and Pulteney replying that he would be satisfied, provided "the main forts of the Government," or, in other words, the principal offices of State, were placed in his hands. It was not till the displacement of Lord North's ministry by that of Lord Rockingham in 1782 that a whole administration, with the exception of the Lord Chancellor, was changed by a vote

of want of confidence passed in the House of Commons. Thenceforth, however, the resignation of the head of a Government in deference to an adverse vote of the popular Chamber has invariably been accompanied by the resignation of all his colleagues. They accept a common responsibility for all his acts of policy, and it is understood that a withdrawal of parliamentary confidence from him implies its withdrawal from them also.

3. *Concert in Action.*—For nearly a century after the Revolution, the Cabinet, instead of being the consentaneously acting body which it is at present, was little more than a loose cluster of mutually independent ministers, carrying on the business of the State in various departments unconnected with each other, and conducting that business under no other general superintendence than that of the Crown. There was no regular concert between ministers : the head of a department was not bound to inform his colleagues, either individually or collectively, of the measures he proposed to take ; nor were there any of these periodical Cabinet Councils in which, nowadays, questions of departmental policy are brought to the cognisance, and sometimes referred to the decision, of the Cabinet at large.

The inconveniences of this system were many, but transition from it to that which now exists did not become possible until the supremacy of the Prime Minister had become an accepted principle of our Government. It was to the want of a recognised chief that this lack of Concert among the Cabinet was due ; yet for a century after the Revolution there was no such recognized chief of the Cabinet even in practice ; nor in theory, it may be added, is there any at the present day. Constitutionally speaking, ministers are all of equal authority as Privy Councillors, the only capacity in which they possess any constitutional authority at all ; and such ascendency as Walpole, for instance, for many years enjoyed was of a purely personal character—the result of his natural capacity for rule. So far indeed was this great parliamentary leader from claiming any supremacy in virtue of his position, that he resented the title of Prime Minister as an imputation, and seemed evidently of opinion that such a functionary would be as hateful to the Englishmen of his day as Clarendon declared it to be to those of his own time. Nor, though he undoubtedly did much to raise that office to the position which it now holds, was he far wrong in his estimate of the opinion then prevailing on the

subject.   It was one of the complaints of the peers who moved an
address to the Crown for his removal, that he had made himself
"sole minister"; and though the motion was defeated, a protest
was afterwards entered in the journals of the House of Lords,
declaring that "a sole or even a First Minister is an officer unknown to the law of Britain, inconsistent with the constitution of
the country, and destructive of liberty in any Government whatsoever"; and further, that "it plainly appearing to us that Sir
Robert Walpole has for many years acted as such by taking upon
himself the chief, if not the sole direction of affairs in the different
branches of the administration, we could not but esteem it to be
an indispensable duty to offer our most humble advice to his
Majesty for the removal of a minister so dangerous to the King
and the kingdoms."   But despite this protest, the office of Prime
Minister continued gradually to attract to itself that "chief if not
sole direction of affairs" which now belongs to it.   The system of
co-ordinate departmental ministers was maintained throughout the
first twenty years of his reign by George III for his own purposes: he "divided" in order to "govern"; but on the accession
of the younger Pitt to power, the King was content to hand over
to him the general superintending authority, which he himself had
hitherto so obstinately struggled to reserve to the Crown.   The
supremacy which this statesman successfully asserted over his
colleagues has ever since been the acknowledged right of the First
Minister of the Crown; and the Constitution, as now practically
interpreted, may be said to proceed uniformly upon the principle
that power and responsibility should be concentrated in the hands
of some one man who enjoys the confidence of the country and the
majority in Parliament. and whose unchallenged authority is
necessary to secure consistency in policy and vigour in administration.

The authority and functions of the Cabinet, and the mutual relations of its component members, are points of so much importance to our present subject, and the history of this body is so
essentially the history of modern executive government in England, that it may be well to recapitulate the successive stages in
its development, as traced in the foregoing pages.

(1.)   First, then, we find the Cabinet appearing in the shape of
a small informal, irregular *Camarilla*, selected at the pleasure of
the Sovereign from the larger body of the Privy Council, consulted

by and privately advising the Crown, but with no power to take any resolutions of State, or perform any act of Government without the assent of the Privy Council, and not as yet even commonly known by its present name. This was its condition anterior to the reign of Charles I.

(2) Then succeeds a second period during which this Council of advice obtains its distinctive title of Cabinet, but without acquiring any recognized status, or *permanently* displacing the Privy Council from its position of *de facto* as well as *de jure* the only authoritative body of advisers of the Crown. (Reign of Charles I and Charles II, the latter of whom governed during a part of his reign by means of a Cabinet, and towards its close through a "reconstructed" Privy Council.)

(3) A third period, commencing with the formation by William III of the first ministry, approaching to the modern type. The Cabinet, though still remaining, as it remains to this day, unknown to the Constitution, has now become *de facto*, though not *de jure*, the real and sole supreme consultative council and executive authority in the State. It is still, however, regarded with jealousy, and the full realisation of the modern constitutional theory of ministerial responsibility, by the admission of its members to a seat in Parliament, is only by degrees effected.

(4) Finally, towards the close of the eighteenth century, the political conception of the Cabinet as a body,—necessarily consisting (*a*) of members of the Legislature (*b*) of the same political views, and chosen from the party possessing a majority in the House of Commons; (*c*) prosecuting a concerted policy; (*d*) under a common responsibility to be signified by collective resignation in the event of parliamentary censure; and (*e*) acknowledging a common subordination to one chief minister, — took definitive shape in our modern theory of the Constitution, and so remains to the present day.

*   *   *   *   *   *   *   *   *

The attention of the reader has already been called to the development of the doctrine of collective ministerial responsibility, and to its constitutional importance ; but it now becomes necessary to note the qualifications to which it is subject. The soundness of the general principle is of course obvious. It is clear enough that so long as it remained possible for a ministry to evade parliamentary condemnation by "throwing overboard" some unlucky colleague, irrespectively of the question whether his acts were or were not in reason and in principle their own acts, the control of Parliament could never be effectively exercised.

"The essence of responsible government," it has been said by an eminent English statesman,* "is that mutual bond of responsibility one for another wherein a government acting by party go together, frame their measures in concert, and where, if one member falls to the ground, the others almost, as a matter of course, fall with him." On the other hand, it would be manifestly as inconvenient as unjust to hold a Government collectively responsible for every administrative blunder committed by an indiscreet or incompetent minister. The rule in such matters appears to be this : that the wrongful acts of a minister in matters peculiarly concerning his own department do not involve the Cabinet at large in any parliamentary censure passed upon such acts, unless (1) they have either voluntarily assumed a share of the responsibility, or (2) are proved, as a matter of fact, to have been implicated in the acts censured. But in cases where the act of an individual minister, though departmental in its nature, is in such consonance with the general policy of the Government that they feel it impossible to repudiate it; or in cases where the retention of such minister in the Cabinet is deemed essential to its existence, and an object to be secured at any cost ; or, lastly, in cases where the act is only departmental *in form*, and is really but a step in the execution of a plan of action already resolved upon by the Cabinet at large ;—in all these cases the responsibility becomes necessarily corporate, and ministry and minister must stand or fall together.

* * * * * * * * *

Lastly, as to the particular measures by which Parliament exercises its powers of calling ministers to account: These divide themselves into ordinary and extraordinary. The ordinary form of procedure resorted to by Parliament against offending ministers is that of censure and dismissal from office ; the extraordinary is that of "impeachment" by the Commons at the bar of the House of Lords. In later times the former has been found sufficient, and it has been the long-settled practice to regard the disapprobation of Parliament and the loss of power as punishment sufficient for all errors of administration committed in good faith and without

---

* The late Lord Derby.

suspicion of corrupt or treasonable motive on the part of the erring ministers. It is indeed nearly a century and a half since the last attempt was made to impeach a minister for merely pursuing a policy considered mischievous by the dominant party in the House of Commons for the time being ; but the much later case of Lord Melville's impeachment for alleged malversation in office shows the indisposition of the House to part with this means of punishing grave and conscious violations of ministerial duty ; and it is not by any means impossible that a detected act of corruption on the part of a minister might, even in these days. expose him to a parliamentary impeachment. Indeed, if it were beyond the reach of the ordinary law, it would have to be so punished, unless the offender were to be allowed entire impunity ; and this consideration, indeed, was the real origin of the process. "The times in which its exercise was needed were those in which the people were jealous of the Crown, when Parliament had less control over prerogative, when courts of justice were impure, and when, instead of vindicating the law, the Crown and its officers resisted its execution, and screened political offenders from justice. But the limitations of prerogative, the immediate responsibility of ministers to Parliament, the vigilance and activity of that body in scrutinising the actions of public men, the settled administration of the law, and the direct influence of Parliament over courts of justice, which are at the same time independent of the Crown, have prevented the consummation of those crimes which impeachments were designed to punish."*

Parliamentary censure of the penal kind,—that. namely, which is followed of necessity by loss of office.— can be pronounced only through the House of Commons. A vote of the Upper House in disapproval of ministerial acts may, and indeed must, carry with it considerable moral weight ; circumstances may be conceived in which its effect might so damage and weaken an administration as to lead ultimately to its downfall ; but it does not amount to "censure" in the constitutional sense of the word. Nothing short of a declared withdrawal of the confidence of the popular Chamber imposes any constitutional obligation upon ministers to resign their offices. This withdrawal of confidence may be signified either by a formal resolution expressive of the fact, or by a vote conveying disapproval of certain specific

---

* May, *Law of Parliament*, p. 374.

acts or omissions on the part of ministers or by the rejection of legislative measures of a certain character introduced by ministers.

The first two cases explain themselves, and with regard to the third—which is much the most usual method of pronouncing parliamentary censure—it is only necessary to note the qualifications attached to it. Not every rejection of a ministerial bill by the House of Commons, not even the rejection of an important bill by them, is regarded as equivalent to, or as intended to convey, a declaration of parliamentary censure. A mere defeat, or even a series of defeats, in the House of Commons upon isolated proposals would not entail the resignation of a Government which had otherwise any ground for believing that its general policy still had the approval of Parliament; nor would the liberal amendment and alteration of measures introduced by ministers of necessity entail their resignation. But if a Government has declared that they regard the passing of a particular measure in a certain shape as a matter of vital importance, the rejection of their advice by the Legislature is tantamount to a vote of want of confidence, and must compel them either to resign or to advise the Sovereign to dissolve Parliament and refer the question to the country. The circumstances in which this advice may be legitimately tendered to the Crown are of various kinds, but the consideration of them belongs to another branch of the subject.

VI

THE TREASURY.—THE BUDGET.

[FROM "CENTRAL GOVERNMENT." BY H. D. TRAILL, IN THE
ENGLISH CITIZEN SERIES."]

IT has been pointed out in the previous chapter that just as "the
Cabinet" has no recognized legal existence, so there is no such
official known to the language of constitutional law as a "Prime
Minister." Supreme as is the authority which the so-called
"Premier" has in course of time established over his colleagues,
and complete as is their subordination to him, he is in theory only
one among other ministers of the Crown, and his sole official title
is derived from the department over which he nominally presides.
This department is nowadays the Treasury, and the office of First
Lord of the Treasury has been held by the Prime Minister, either
alone or in conjunction with another, ever since the year 1806.
His position, however, in relation to the internal economy of this
department is rather of honorary president than of working
chief; and he is usually too much occupied in considering questions of the general administrative and legislative policy of the
country to have time to attend to the departmental business of the
office. This business is principally transacted by the other members of the Treasury Board, an institution to whose historical
origin it will here be convenient to devote a few words.

The full official description of the persons who constitute this
Board is that of "Lords Commissioners for executing the office of
Lord High Treasurer," the said persons being the First Lord of
the Treasury, the Chancellor of the Exchequer, and three other
officials known as "Junior Lords."

The Lord High Treasurer was anciently the sole head of the
Treasury, and the most powerful minister in England. For more
than a century and a half, however, this high office has been
placed, as it is called, "in commission." The Duke of Shrewsbury
had been appointed Lord High Treasurer by Queen Anne a day or
two before her death; but George I, a few months after his

accession, nominated Lord Halifax and four other persons "Lords
Commissioners for executing the office of Lord High Treasurer,"
and the office has continued in commission ever since. The
Treasury, however, has undergone the same sort of centralizing
process as the Cabinet; for while the Commissioners appointed
in earlier times for the execution of this office were, it would seem,
of co-ordinate authority, and nominated by the Crown, they have
ever since 1715 been appointed by, dependent upon, and subordinate to, the First Lord.   For a considerable time, however, they
continued to take a real and active part in the administrative
business of the department; and it was only by degrees that their
offices declined into the virtual sinecures which (in a departmental
though by no means in a parliamentary sense) they have now
become.   The Treasury is still a board of commissioners in name,
and the patent under which the members of the Board are appointed still represents them as being of equal authority, with
powers to any two or more of them to discharge the functions of
the whole.   But the Treasury has long since ceased to be a Board
in anything but name: it is now practically a department pre-
sided over by a single head, the Chancellor of the Exchequer.

*   *   *   *   *   *   *   *   *

We have now to trace the change by which this minister has
gradually concentrated the collective authority of the Treasury
Board in his own hands.   Originally, when the business of the
Treasury was much smaller than it is at present, it was really
transacted by the Board in presence of the Sovereign.   The First
Lord, the Chancellor of the Exchequer, and the Junior Lords,
used to sit at the table; the secretaries attended with their
papers, which they read, and the Sovereign and the Lords gave
their opinions thereon, the secretaries taking notes of the
proceedings, which were afterwards drawn up in the shape
of minutes and read at the next Board meeting.   The increase of business, however, during the later years of the last century rendered it impossible to dispose of the business of the
Treasury in this way; and it then came to be transacted on the
principle of individual responsibility.   Papers were still read and
passed at Board meetings, to preserve regularity and to comply
with the directions of certain acts of Parliament; but the Board
soon ceased to be a reality.   The business was transacted by the
junior members, the secretaries, and the permanent officials, under
responsibility to the Chancellor of the Exchequer and the First

Lord of the Treasury. Then after a time these functionaries ceased to meet the Board, except on extraordinary occasions; and some thirty years ago the Board itself ceased to meet. The Junior Lords of the Treasury are virtually set aside, and have no regular departmental duty to perform, except of a mere routine description, such as signing documents for which their signature is legally necessary; and the real business of the department is transacted by the secretary and the permanent officials, under the direction and control of the Chancellor of the Exchequer.

It was the ancient duty of the Lord High Treasurer, or of the commissioners for executing his office, to "provide and take care of the King's profit"; and the Treasury, with the Chancellor of the Exchequer at its head, discharges, as the successor to this duty, exceedingly extensive and important functions.

They are:—

(1) To provide the means of meeting the necessary yearly expenditure on the military, naval, and civil services of the nation.

(2) To exercise a certain control and supervision (the nature of which will be shortly indicated) over the amount and details of that expenditure.

(3) To revise and regulate the internal or domestic expenditure of the other public offices of the State; and generally to exercise such a superintendent authority over the financial management of these offices as is implied in these revisory and regulative powers.

(4) To decide upon appeals from its own subordinate departments, in all cases arising out of the receipt of revenue; and

(5) To determine as to the remission of fines and forfeitures to the Crown.

It is, however, the first of these duties—that, namely, of introducing what is called "The Budget"—with which the name and office of the Chancellor of the Exchequer is most familiarly associated; and it will be here convenient to give a brief explanation of this important constitutional proceeding.

But before considering the mode of raising the funds required for defraying the annual expenditure of the State, it would be only natural to inquire how the amount of that expenditure is determined. The two operations, though both alike of a financial nature, are obviously quite distinct; and though each is performed by the whole House of Commons, the Committee into which the

House resolves itself for each purpose is described in each case by a distinct name. It is in what is called "Committee of Supply" that the House determines what sums of money are sufficient to meet the annual expenditure of the State, and votes them as "supplies" to the Crown for employment upon that object; it is in Committee of "Ways and Means" that it considers and approves the means suggested for raising, by taxation, or otherwise, the sums required.

The first step in the former process is the "presentation of estimates." Shortly after the meeting of Parliament and the opening of the Committee of Supply, the ministers in charge of the naval and military services lay before the Committee their respective statements of the sums which will be required for the maintenance of those services ; and somewhat later in the session a common estimate for the various civil services is submitted also. These estimates are presented to the House, it should be noted, *on the collective responsibility of the whole Cabinet*. It is the duty of the heads of the respective departments to which they relate to explain such matters to the Committee as may satisfy them of the correctness of the calculations relied upon, and formally to move that the sum required for each item of expenditure should be voted ; but the Cabinet, as a whole, is responsible for the demand. Indeed, the Army and Navy Estimates have, as a rule, been considered and settled in Cabinet Council before being submitted to the House ; and the collective responsibility of the ministry is in this case, therefore, not technical merely, but substantial. But the Chancellor of the Exchequer, over and above his share in this common responsibility, has in his Departmental capacity a special concern in this matter. It is his duty to satisfy himself that the estimates have been framed with due regard to economy ; and though the heads of the military and naval departments must necessarily have entire freedom of judgment as to the needs of their respective services, it would still be the duty of the Chancellor of the Exchequer to disallow any expenditure which he might think unnecessary or inordinate, and in the event, which rarely happens, of an item being pressed, in the face of the objection of the Treasury, to oppose it in the Cabinet.

In order to a more effective exercise of this control, a circular is, in the autumn of every year, addressed by the Treasury to the various departments of the Government, including the naval and military establishments, requesting that, by a certain date, an estimate of the sums required by the particular department for the service of the current year may be prepared for the information of the Treasury. The estimates are called for thus early in order to afford time to the Chancellor to examine them thoroughly, with two distinct objects in view,—one, that of keeping down expenditure within legitimate limits, and the other, that of ascertaining as early as may be how much expenditure within these limits it will be his duty to provide for.

Suppose, then, that the estimates for the various services have been duly examined and approved, the Chancellor of the Exchequer has now to consider how the demands of these estimates are to be met. The first question, of course, is whether the income of the State for the ensuing year will be sufficient to cover them, or, if not, how far it will fall short of their amount. The next step, therefore, is to ascertain what the next year's income of the State may be expected to amount to; and with this object the Chancellor of the Exchequer obtains from the permanent heads of the revenue departments their estimates of the public revenue for the ensuing year upon the hypothesis that taxation will remain unchanged.

Let us now first assume that these estimates, on a comparison with the estimates of expenditure. are found to exceed them by a more or less considerable sum. In this case there is said to be a *surplus*—a word which, it must be noted, is as a rule used in a *prospective* sense in finance, and as meaning not the national balance in hand after payment of national charges, but simply *excess of estimated revenue over estimated expenditure.* Should this excess of revenue be considerable, the Government will, as a rule, decide that the greater portion of such excess shall not be collected at all, but that taxation to the extent of that amount shall be remitted. In such a* case it would be for the Chancellor of the Exchequer, in the first instance, to make choice of the particular imposts which he considers should be abolished or reduced; and when his selection has been approved by the Cabinet, all is ready for the introduction of his budget. Accordingly, at or soon before the close of the financial year (the national accounts being made up on the 5th of April), he submits to the House of Commons a general statement of the results of the financial measures of the preceding session; he gives a general view of the expected income and expenditure for the ensuing year; and having thus made the House acquainted with the amount of the expected surplus at his disposal, he indicates the particular remissions of taxation by which he proposes to dispose of it. These proposals, after all questions which may be put with respect to them by members of the House have been answered by the Chancellor of the Exchequer, are then embodied in resolutions; and these resolutions, when afterwards reported to the House, form the groundwork of bills for accomplishing the contemplated changes. The House can, of course, either express disapproval of the budget as a whole, or oppose, and perhaps reject, any one of the resolutions which accompany it. Ministers have, on not a few occasions, suffered defeats of this kind; and it depends upon circumstances, which will be briefly considered hereafter, whether in such a case they would deem it proper to submit to their defeat, and withdraw or modify their condemned proposals, or treat the adverse vote of the House as a withdrawal of its confidence, and resign their offices.

If, on the other hand, a comparison of the estimates of revenue and expenditure discloses an excess of the latter over the former, the Chancellor of the Exchequer will, of course, have not a *surplus* to dispose of but a *deficit* to make good; and he will have to devise means of meeting it, whether by loan or by increased taxation. If the latter expedient is, as usually happens, adopted, he will have to consider what existing taxes should be augmented, or what new taxes imposed; and, after obtaining the approval of the Cabinet to his proposals, he will submit them as before, along with his general financial statement, to the House of Commons. There they will be subjected to the same criticism, and, if not regarded as a satisfactory mode of meeting the deficit, they may be set aside in favour of alternative schemes, or they may be simply rejected out of hand. The House is in no way bound to grant the demands of a Government for the means of meeting a deficiency, although, of course, the unqualified refusal of such a demand, without the suggestion of any alternative, would be equivalent to a vote of "no confidence" of the most emphatic kind.

Should the national accounts disclose a surplus of only trifling amount, it would probably be left undisposed of, as a margin against possible error in the estimates of expenditure or of revenue; and in this case, as also in the case of an absolute equilibrium being established between expenditure and revenue, the duty of the Chancellor of the Exchequer will be confined to the proposal of such readjustments of taxation—such transfers of taxes, that is to say, from one class of tax-payers to another—as he may conceive to tend to a more equitable distribution of public burdens, or to conduce, by the relief of particular industries, to the increased prosperity of the country. But in all cases where the surplus is considerable, it would, as a general rule, be the duty of the Chancellor of the Exchequer to dispose of it, and of the House of Commons to see that he does so ; for the effect of a budget is to satisfy Parliament not only that the public income to be raised for the current financial year will be sufficient, but that it will be no more than sufficient, to meet the expenditure which the Government propose to incur within that year. To raise more revenue than is required is simply to lock up in the Exchequer so much money that might, to the greater advantage of the country, have been left to "fructify," as the phrase is, "in the pockets of the people."

Thus far, however, we have been dealing only with *proposals*,—with proposals on the one hand to spend so much money, and on the other hand to raise so much money ; and we have now to consider the process by which the actual payments into and out of the National Exchequer are effected. The *local* details of the collection of revenue are obviously foreign to the subject of this volume. and the public moneys cannot be held to come within the scope of its inquiries until they are actually lodged in the coffers of the Central Government. These moneys which consist partly of the hereditary revenues of the Crown (now surrendered to the control of Parliament in exchange for the Civil List), and partly of the proceeds of taxation, are nowadays all alike paid into the Banks of England and Ireland "to the account of the Exchequer," and constitute one common fund known as *the Consolidated Fund*. It is out of this fund that the payments for the services of the country are, upon proper authority, made ; and the nature and conditions of this authority next claim consideration.

It is of two kinds : one of a permanent character, and the other dependent upon periodical exercise of the power of Parliament ; and more than half of the money is dealt with under authority of the former kind. About three-fifths of the whole annual expenditure is made under the express direction of Acts of

Parliament, and these payments can be made, therefore, without the sanction of a special parliamentary vote.   The interest on the National debt, the sums payable for the Civil List, annuities to the royal family, pensions, certain salaries and allowances, the expenses of the courts of justice,—these, together with certain other charges, unnecessary to enumerate, are imposed by permanent statute upon the Consolidated Fund ; and these statutes are, of course, a sufficient authority to the custodians of the Fund to make the several payments required.   The principle represented in this procedure is that the security of the public creditor, the dignity of the Crown, the independence of judges, etc., are objects of public concern ; and that these objects would be imperfectly attained if the payments above enumerated were subjected to the uncertainty of an annual vote.

But as regards the remaining two-fifths of the expenditure, which includes interest on the *unfunded* debt, the maintenance of the naval and military forces, the expenses of the collection of revenue, and the charges of the various civil services, no payments can be made under these several heads except on the authority of express parliamentary votes.

The process, however, by which this authority is obtained is a somewhat complex one, and the various forms and securities by which the outgoings of the public Exchequer are constitutionally regulated are elaborate enough to require a few words of detailed explanation.

The mode in which the sanction of Parliament is obtained for the various proposals of expenditure submitted by ministers in their estimates has already been explained in the brief account given above of the proceedings in Committee of Supply ; but another process is necessary before this parliamentary sanction can be made practically available by the Executive.   A vote in Supply is a mere resolution of the House of Commons that certain sums of national money shall be appropriated to certain national purposes ; it gives no authority to the Government to draw upon the Exchequer, nor to the Custodian of the revenues—the Comptroller of the Exchequer—to make any payments or advances thereout.   Such a resolution merely authorises the expenditure, but does not provide the means of making it.   To make this provision the functions of another committee—the Committee of Ways and Means—require to be called into play.   Accordingly, as soon as the votes on account of the great services have been "reported," a resolution is proposed in Committee of Ways and Means for a general grant out of the Consolidated Fund "towards making good the supply granted to Her Majesty"; and the principle of parliamentary control is so strictly respected that the grant is never allowed to exceed the amount of the votes actually passed in Committee of Supply. Even then, however, the process is not constitutionally complete, for the Constitution requires the assent of the Crown and the House of Lords to the appropriation of public moneys; and the resolution of the Committee of Ways and Means has therefore to be embodied in a Bill, which passes through its various stages, and at a very early period of the session receives the royal assent; at which time, but not before, the Treasury acquires full power to direct an issue out of the Consolidated Fund to meet the payments authorised by the votes in Supply, or, if that Fund be insufficient, to raise by Exchequer Bills, on the security of the Fund, the money required to defray the expenditure sanctioned by such votes.

* * * * * * * * *

The control of Parliament over the expenditure of public money being thus rendered as complete in detail as it is in gross, it is natural to inquire how the exercise of so rigorous and minute a restraint can be made consistent with the always varying needs and often recurring emergencies of the public service. How, it will be asked, is a Government to provide for expenditure suddenly necessitated by cases like these, and the necessity for which may arise at a time when Parliament is not in session, and there is consequently no possibility of obtaining even the sanction of a vote in Supply, to say nothing of the more precise authority of an Appropriation Act? The answer to this is, that the Legislature has already created certain permanent funds applicable to such contingencies, and the Executive is invested with permanent statutory powers of resorting to them. To meet the needs of the public service, more particularly in the colonies and at the various naval and military stations of the empire, the Government is authorised to make advances, as occasion arises, out of a fund called the Treasury Chest Fund, which by the Act 24 and 25 Vict. c. 127, is limited to £1,300,000, and assigned for employment by the Treasury as "a banking fund for facilitating remittances, and for temporary advances for public and colonial services, to be repaid out of the moneys appropriated by Parliament, or otherwise applicable to those services." There is also another and smaller fund, called the Civil Contingencies Fund, limited to £120,000, on which the Treasury is empowered to draw from time to time to defray new and unforeseen expenditure for civil services at home, for which no votes had been taken, or to meet deficiencies on ordinary votes. Every advance made from these funds must, however, be repaid out of the parliamentary votes passed in the ensuing year to provide for the services for which such advances had been made ; and no expenditure whatever is allowed to become a final charge upon these funds, which are thus, after each successive call is made upon them, restored to their statutory maximum.

The restraints and privileges which have been discussed in, the foregoing pages have reference to the Treasury only in its capacity as superintendent of the actual work of administration, and for that purpose an expender of public money ; but the Treasury exercises, it has been said, a function of scarcely less importance than that of directing the national outlay, in scrutinising, checking, and confining within economical bounds, the domestic expenditure, as it may be called, of the various departments. The Chancellor of the Exchequer, in other words, is not only the head, so to speak, of the national counting-house,—he is the housekeeper of the national household. The control of the Treasury over the other departments of State rests not only upon long usage and tradition, but on express recommendations of Parliament, and indeed on the economical principle that there ought to be one authority responsible to Parliament for every act of internal departmental expenditure. Accordingly we find a constant and minute supervision exercised in the name of "My Lords" of the Treasury over all the pecuniary incidents of the management of the various public offices. A "minute of the Treasury" is required for the sanction of any changes in the *personnel* of their working staff, or any redistribution of their duties which may involve the outlay of public money ; and it is the custom to append to the annual estimates any correspondence which may have taken place between the Treasury and other departments upon any questions connected either with their internal or external expenditure which may be deemed sufficiently important to be brought under the notice of Parliament.

THE TREASURY.—THE BUDGET.   87

The parliamentary responsibility of this department is, as becomes its importance, provided for with exceptional completeness. Its working chief, as has been said, belongs as a matter of course to the Lower House of Parliament, and can therefore be called to account by interrogation or motion with respect to all matters of Treasury concern, which, as we know, include a variety of questions that may arise in any of the other departments of the State, and may in fact be said to cover the whole sphere of the discipline and economy of the Executive Government. And not only does the invariable presence of the Chancellor of the Exchequer in the House of Commons make the representation of this department peculiarly direct, but, through the Secretary of the Treasury, and, with respect to certain departmental matters, through the Junior Lords, the House possesses peculiar facilities of ascertaining and expressing its opinion upon the details of Treasury administration. This is especially the case as regards the Secretary of the Treasury, whose functions have greatly increased of late years, and whose office has now become perhaps the most important of any not included in the Cabinet. These officials, however, do not of course relieve their chief of any share of his official responsibility; nor would they do so, indeed, if they constituted the sole representatives of their department in the popular House, instead of being mere attendants therein upon their chief.

A word should be said here as to the constitutional position of such officials in general. An Under Secretary or other subordinate minister must be regarded as being merely the mouthpiece of his superior officer, and as only responsible for giving effect to the instructions of his chief, and for personal good behaviour. The political head of the department is alone responsible to Parliament. This proposition is substantially true, even in those cases in which an Under Secretary represents his department in one House, while his chief sits in another. It is true that an Under Secretary or a Vice-President, who is in this position, and is required to take a prominent part in public affairs, "is naturally supposed to have a share in the government of the department, and cannot absolve himself from a certain modified responsibility in regard to it"; but a "much greater responsibility attaches to the departmental chief whose directions the subordinate officer is obliged to carry out, and whose authority is supreme." On the whole, in short, it may be said with practical accuracy, that the head of the department is "alone" responsible ; and that however influential a position his subordinate might occupy in virtue of his representing that department in the House of Commons, it is doubtful whether he could in any case become *constitutionally bound* (although, of course, he might personally prefer) to accept a parliamentary censure on a point of departmental policy as applicable to himself as well as his chief. That such censure can ever apply to himself alone, and to the exclusion of his chief, may be confidently pronounced impossible ; the only (apparent) instance to the contrary will be dealt with in its proper place.

The position of these subordinate officials must be borne in mind in noting what may be said hereafter on the subject of departmental responsibility. In cases where the head of a department is usually or frequently a member of the House of Lords, the parliamentary responsibility of that department is in common parlance spoken of as being provided for by the presence of this or the other departmental official in the House of Commons. Nor does there seem any objection to the expression, so long as we take care not to forget that such officials represent not the principle of responsibility, but an incidental part of the machinery for giving effect to that principle ; that their position is that of mere intermediaries between the chiefs of departments and the popular assembly to which these chiefs are responsible, keeping the House duly informed of all that the minister has done, explaining and justifying his proceedings when necessary, and receiving vicariously the censure or the approval which the House thinks proper to pronounce thereon.

In the case, then, of the *internal* administration of the Treasury, whether in its dealings with its subordinate departments of revenue, or as regards the exercise of its economical supervision over the other offices of the State, the sole responsibility rests upon the Chancellor of the Exchequer. In respect of the *general financial policy* proposed by this official, he shares responsibility, as has been said, with the Cabinet at large. And as regards this policy, it should here be noted that a somewhat wider latitude of submission to parliamentary disapproval, without resigning office, is allowed to ministers in respect to questions of taxation and finance. The doctrine laid down on this point by more than one eminent political authority, and generally accepted as sound, is, that questions of taxation "are questions upon which the House of Commons, representing the country, have peculiar claims to have their opinions listened to, and upon which the Executive Government may very fairly, without any loss of dignity,—provided they maintain a sufficient revenue for the credit of the country and for its establishments,—reconsider any particular measure of finance they have proposed." This, however, as indeed is to be inferred from the proviso with which Lord John Russell qualified the above remarks, applies only to the questions of "ways and means," and not to "questions of supply." A Government, in other words, may legitimately submit to the rejection of a proposal to raise a particular sum of money in a particular way; but they cannot acquiesce in a refusal on the part of Parliament to sanction the expenditure which ministers have assumed the responsibility of declaring necessary for the support of the Civil Government, and the maintenance of the public credit at home and abroad. "No Government," says one of the greatest of authorities on financial administration, "could be worthy of its place if it permitted its estimates to be seriously resisted by the Opposition; and important changes can be made therein only under circumstances which permit of the raising of the question of a change of Government."

VII.

CHANGES OF MINISTRY.

[From Bagehot's "English Constitution."]

THERE is one error as to the English Constitution which crops up periodically. Circumstances which often, though irregularly, occur naturally suggest that error, and as surely as they happen it revives. The relation of Parliament, and especially of the House of Commons, to the Executive Government is the specific peculiarity of our constitution, and an event which frequently happens much puzzles some people as to it.

That event is a change of ministry. All our administrators go out together. The whole executive government changes—at least, all the heads of it change in a body, and at every such change some speculators are sure to exclaim that such a habit is foolish. They say, "No doubt Mr. Gladstone and Lord Russell may have been wrong about Reform; no doubt Mr. Gladstone may have been cross in the House of Commons; but why should either or both of these events change all the heads of all our practical departments? What could be more absurd than what happened in 1858? Lord Palmerston was for once in his life over-buoyant; he gave rude answers to stupid enquiries; he brought into the Cabinet a nobleman concerned in an ugly trial about a woman; he, or his Foreign Secretary, did not answer a French despatch by a despatch, but told our ambassador to reply orally. And because of these trifles, or at any rate these isolated *unadministrative* mistakes, all our administration had fresh heads. The Poor Law Board had a new chief, the Home Department a new chief, the Public Works a new chief. Surely this was absurd." Now, is this objection good or bad? Speaking generally, is it wise so to change all our rulers?

The practice produces three great evils. First, it brings in on a sudden new persons and untried persons to preside over our policy. A little while ago Lord Cranborne* had no more idea

---

* Now Lord Salisbury, who, when this was written, was Indian Secretary.—*Note* to second edition.

that he would now be Indian Secretary than that he would be a bill broker. He had never given any attention to Indian affairs ; he can get them up, because he is an able, educated man who can get up anything. But they are not "part and parcel" of his mind ; not his subjects of familiar reflection, nor things of which he thinks by predilection, of which he cannot help thinking. But because Lord Russell and Mr. Gladstone did not please the House of Commons about Reform, there he is. A perfectly inexperienced man, so far as Indian affairs go, rules all our Indian empire. And if all our heads of offices change together, so very frequently it must be. If twenty offices are vacant at once, there are almost never twenty tried, competent, clever men ready to take them. The difficulty of making up a government is very much like the difficulty of putting together a Chinese puzzle : the spaces do not suit what you have to put into them. And the difficulty of matching a ministry is more than that of fitting a puzzle, because the ministers to be put in can object, though the bits of a puzzle cannot. One objector can throw out the combination. In 1847 Lord Grey would not join Lord John Russell's projected government if Lord Palmerston was to be Foreign Secretary ; Lord Palmerston *would* be Foreign Secretary, and so the government was not formed. The cases in which a single refusal prevents a government are rare, and there must be many concurrent circumstances to make it effectual. But the cases in which refusals impair or spoil a government are very common. It almost never happens that the ministry-maker can put into his offices exactly whom he would like ; a number of placemen are always too proud, too eager, or too obstinate to go just where they should.

Again, this system not only makes new ministers ignorant, but keeps present ministers indifferent. A man cannot feel the same interest that he might in his work if he knows that by events over which he has no control,—by errors in which he had no share,— by metamorphoses of opinion, which belong to a different sequence of phenomena, he may have to leave that work in the middle, and may very likely never return to it. The new man put into a fresh office ought to have the best motive to learn his task thoroughly, but, in fact, in England, he has not at all the best motive. The last wave of party and politics brought him there, the next may take him away. Young and eager men take, even at this dis-

advantage, a keen interest in office work, but most men, especially
old men, hardly do so. Many a battered minister may be seen to
think much more of the vicissitudes which make him and unmake
him, than of any office matter.

Lastly, a sudden change of ministers may easily cause a mischievous change of policy. In many matters of business, perhaps
in most, a continuity of mediocrity is better than a hotch-potch of
excellences. For example, now that the progress in the scientific
arts is revolutionising the instruments of war, rapid changes in
our head-preparers for land and sea war are most costly and most
hurtful. A single competent selector of new inventions would
probably in the course of years, after some experience, arrive at
something tolerable; it is in the nature of steady, regular, ex-
perimenting ability to diminish, if not vanquish, such difficulties.
But a quick succession of chiefs has no similar facility. They do
not learn from each others' experience;—you might as well expect
the new head boy at a public school to learn from the experience
of the last head boy. The most valuable result of many years is
a nicely-balanced mind instinctively heedful of various errors;
but such a mind is the incommunicable gift of individual experience, and an outgoing minister can no more leave it to his
successor, than an elder brother can pass it on to a younger.
Thus a desultory and incalculable policy may follow from a rapid
change of ministers.

These are formidable arguments, but four things may, I think,
be said in reply to, or mitigation of them. A little examination
will show that this change of ministers is essential to a Parliamentary government;—that something like it will happen in all
elective governments, and that worse happens under presidential
government;—that it is not necessarily prejudicial to a good
administration, but that, on the contrary, something like it is a
prerequisite of good administration;—that the evident evils of
English administration are not the results of Parliamentary government, but of grave deficiencies in other parts of our political
and social state;—that, in a word, they result not from what we
have, but from what we have *not*.

As to the first point, those who wish to remove the choice of
ministers from Parliament have not adequately considered what a
Parliament is. A Parliament is nothing less than a big meeting
of more or less idle people. In proportion as you give it power

it will enquire into everything, settle everything, meddle in every-thing. In an ordinary despotism, the powers of a despot are limited by his bodily capacity, and by the calls of pleasure; he is but one man;—there are but twelve hours in his day, and he is not disposed to employ more than a small part in dull business;—he keeps the rest for the court, or the harem, or for society. He is at the top of the world, and all the pleasures of the world are set before him. Mostly there is only a very small part of political business which he cares to understand, and much of it (with the shrewd sensual sense belonging to the race) he knows that he will never understand. But a Parliament is composed of a great number of men by no means at the top of the world. When you establish a predominant Parliament, you give over the rule of the country to a despot who has unlimited time,—who has unlimited vanity,—who has, or believes he has, unlimited comprehension, whose pleasure is in action, whose life is work. There is no limit to the curiosity of Parliament. Sir Robert Peel once suggested that a list should be taken down of the questions asked of him in a single evening; they touched more or less on fifty subjects, and there were a thousand other subjects which by parity of reason might have been added too. As soon as bore A ends, bore B begins. Some enquire from genuine love of knowledge, or from a real wish to improve what they ask about,—others to see their names in the papers,—others to show a watchful constituency that they are alert,—others to get on and to get a place in the govern-ment,—others from an accumulation of little motives they could not themselves analyse, or because it is their habit to ask things. And a proper reply must be given. It was said that "Darby Griffith destroyed Lord Palmerston's first Government," and undoubtedly the cheerful impertinence with which in the conceit of victory that minister answered grave men much hurt his Par-liamentary power. There is one thing which no one will permit to be treated lightly,—himself. And so there is one too which a sovereign assembly will never permit to be lessened or ridiculed, —its own power. The minister of the day will have to give an account in Parliament of all branches of administration, to say why they act when they do, and why they do not when they don't.

Nor is chance enquiry all a public department has most to fear. Fifty members of Parliament may be zealous for a particular policy affecting the department, and fifty others for another policy,

and between them they may divide its action, spoil its favourite
aims, and prevent its consistently working out either of their own
aims. The process is very simple. Every department at times
looks as if it was in a scrape; some apparent blunder, perhaps
some real blunder, catches the public eye. At once the antago-
nist Parliamentary sections, which want to act on the department,
seize the opportunity. They make speeches, they move for documents, they amass statistics. They declare "that in no other
country is such a policy possible as that which the department is
pursuing; that it is mediæval; that it costs money; that it wastes
life; that America does the contrary; that Prussia does the contrary." The newspapers follow according to their nature. These
bits of administrative scandal amuse the public. Articles on them
are very easy to write, easy to read, easy to talk about. They
please the vanity of mankind. We think as we read, "Thank
God, *I* am not as that man; *I* did not send green coffee to the
Crimea; *I* did not send patent cartridge to the common guns, and
common cartridge to the breech loaders. *I* make money; that
miserable public functionary only wastes money." As for the
defence of the department, no one cares for it or reads it. Naturally at first hearing it does not sound true. The opposition
have the unrestricted selection of the point of attack, and they
seldom choose a case in which the department, upon the surface
of the matter, seems to be right. The case of first impression
will always be that something shameful has happened; that such
and such men did die; that this and that gun would not go off;
that this or that ship will not sail. All the pretty reading is
unfavourable, and all the praise is very dull.

Nothing is more helpless than such a department in Parliament
if it has no authorised official defender. The wasps of the House
fasten on it; here they perceive is something easy to sting, and
safe, for it cannot sting in return. The small grain of foundation
for complaint germinates till it becomes a whole crop. At once
the minister of the day is appealed to; he is at the head of
the administration, and he must put the errors right, if such they
are. The opposition leader says, "I put it to the right honourable gentleman, the First Lord of the Treasury. He is a man of
business. I do not agree with him in his choice of ends, but he
is an almost perfect master of methods and means. What he
wishes to do he does do. Now I appeal to him whether such

gratuitous errors, such fatuous incapacity, are to be permitted in
the public service. Perhaps the right honourable gentleman will
grant me his attention while I show from the very documents
of the department," &c., &c. What is the minister to do? He
never heard of this matter; he does not care about the matter.
Several of the supporters of the Government are interested in the
opposition to the department; a grave man, supposed to be wise,
mutters, "This is too bad." The Secretary of the Treasury tells
him, "The House is uneasy. A good many men are shaky. A.
B. said yesterday he had been dragged through the dirt four nights
following. Indeed I am disposed to think myself that the department has been somewhat lax. Perhaps an enquiry," &c., &c.
And upon that the Prime Minister rises and says, "That Her
Majesty's Government having given very serious and grave consideration to this most important subject, are not prepared to say
that in so complicated a matter the department has been perfectly
exempt from error. He does not indeed concur in all the statements which have been made; it is obvious that several of the
charges advanced are inconsistent with one another. If A. had
really died from eating green coffee on the Tuesday, it is plain he
could not have suffered from insufficient medical attendance on the
following Thursday. However, on so complex a subject, and one
so foreign to common experience, he will not give a judgment.
And if the honourable member would be satisfied with having the
matter enquired into by a committee of that House, he will be
prepared to accede to the suggestion."

Possibly the outlying department, distrusting the ministry,
crams a friend. But it is happy indeed if it chances on a judicious friend. The persons most ready to take up that sort of
business are benevolent amateurs, very well intentioned, very
grave, very respectable, but also rather dull. Their words are
good, but about the joints their arguments are weak. They speak
very well, but while they are speaking the decorum is so great
that everybody goes away. Such a man is no match for a couple
of House of Commons gladiators. They pull what he says to
shreds. They show or say that he is wrong about his facts. Then
he rises in a fuss and must explain: but in his hurry he mistakes,
and cannot find the right paper, and becomes first hot, then confused, next inaudible, and so sits down. Probably he leaves the
House with the notion that the defence of the department has

broken down, and so the *Times* announces to all the world as soon
as it awakes.

Some thinkers have naturally suggested that the heads of departments should as such have the right of speech in the House.
But the system when it has been tried has not answered. M.
Guizot tells us from his own experience that such a system is not
effectual. A great popular assembly has a corporate character ; it
has its own privileges, prejudices, and notions. And one of these
notions is that its own members—the persons it sees every day—
whose qualities it knows, whose minds it can test, are those whom
it can most trust. A clerk speaking from without would be an
unfamiliar object. He would be an outsider. He would speak
under suspicion ; he would speak without dignity. Very often he
would speak as a victim. All the bores of the House would be
upon him. He would be put upon examination. He would have
to answer interrogatories. He would be put through the figures
and cross-questioned in detail. The whole effect of what he said
would be lost in *quæstiunculæ* and hidden in a controversial
detritus.

Again, such a person would rarely speak with great ability.
He would speak as a scribe. His habits must have been formed
in the quiet of an office ; he is used to red tape, placidity, and the
respect of subordinates. Such a person will hardly ever be able
to stand the hurly-burly of a public assembly. He will lose his
head—he will say what he should not. He will get hot and red ;
he will feel he is a sort of culprit. After being used to the flat-
tering deference of deferential subordinates, he will be pestered
by fuss and confounded by invective. He will hate the House as
naturally as the House does not like him. He will be an incompetent speaker addressing a hostile audience.

And what is more, an outside administrator addressing Parliament can move Parliament only by the goodness of his arguments.
He has no votes to back them up with. He is sure to be at
chronic war with some active minority of assailants or others.
The natural mode in which a department is improved on great
points and new points is by external suggestion ; the worse foes
of a department are the plausible errors which the most visible
facts suggest, and which only half visible facts confute. Both
the good ideas and the bad ideas are sure to find advocates first
in the press and then in Parliament. Against these a permanent

clerk would have to contend by argument alone. The Minister, the head of the parliamentary Government, will not care for him. The Minister will say in some undress soliloquy, "These permanent 'fellows' must look after themselves. I cannot be bothered. I have only a majority of nine, and a very shaky majority, too. I cannot afford to make enemies for those whom I did not appoint. They did nothing for me, and I can do nothing for them." And if the permanent clerk come to ask his help, he will say in decorous language, "I am sure that if the department can evince to the satisfaction of Parliament that its past management has been such as the public interests require, no one will be more gratified than myself. I am not aware if it will be in my power to attend in my place on Monday ; but if I can be so fortunate, I shall listen to your official statement with my very best attention." And so the permanent public servant will be teased by the wits, oppressed by the bores, and massacred by the innovators of Parliament.

The incessant tyranny of Parliament over the public offices is prevented and can only be prevented by the appointment of a parliamentary head, connected by close ties with the present ministry and the ruling party in Parliament. The parliamentary head is a protecting machine. He and the friends he brings stand between the department and the busybodies and crotchetmakers of the House and the country. So long as at any moment the policy of an office could be altered by chance votes in either House of Parliament, there is no security for any consistency. Our guns and our ships are not, perhaps. very good now. But they would be much worse if any thirty or forty advocates for this gun or that gun could make a motion in Parliament, beat the department, and get their ships or their guns adopted. The "Black Breech Ordnance Company" and the "Adamantine Ship Company" would soon find representatives in Parliament, if forty or fifty members would get the national custom for their rubbish. But this result is now prevented by the parliamentary head of the department. As soon as the Opposition begins the attack, he looks up his means of defence. He studies the subject, compiles his arguments, and builds little piles of statistics, which he hopes will have some effect. He has his reputation at stake, and he wishes to show that he is worth his present place, and fit for future promotion. He is well known, perhaps liked, by the House

—at any rate the House attends to him; he is one of the regular speakers whom they hear and heed. He is sure to be able to get himself heard, and he is sure to make the best defence he can. And after he has settled his speech he loiters up to the Secretary of the Treasury, and says quietly, "They have got a motion against me on Tuesday, you know. I hope you will have your men here. A lot of fellows have crotchets and though they do not agree a bit with one another, they are all against the department; they will all vote for the enquiry." And the Secretary answers, "Tuesday, you say; no (looking at a paper), I do not think it will come on on Tuesday. There is Higgins on Education. He is good for a long time. But anyhow it shall be all right." And then he glides about and speaks a word here and a word there, in consequence of which, when the anti-official motion is made, a considerable array of steady, grave faces sits behind the Treasury Bench—nay, possibly a rising man who sits in outlying independence below the gangway rises to defend the transaction; the department wins by thirty-three, and the management of that business pursues its steady way.

This contrast is no fancy picture. The experiment of conducting the administration of a public department by an independent unsheltered authority has often been tried, and always failed. Parliament always poked at it, till it made it impossible. The most remarkable is that of the Poor Law. The administration of that law is not now very good, but it is not too much to say that almost the whole of its goodness has been preserved by its having an official and party protector in the House of Commons. Without that contrivance we should have drifted back into the errors of the old Poor Law, and superadded to them the present meanness and incompetence in our large towns. All would have been given up to local management. Parliament would have interfered with the central board till it made it impotent, and the local authorities would have been despotic. The first administration of the new Poor Law was by "Commissioners"—the three kings of Somerset House, as they were called. The system was certainly not tried in untrustworthy hands. At the crisis Mr. Chadwick, one of the most active and best administrators in England, was the secretary and the motive power: the principal Commissioner was Sir George Lewis, perhaps the best selective administrator of our time. But the House of Commons would not let the Commission alone. For a long time it was defended because the Whigs had made the Commission, and felt bound as a party to protect it. The new law started upon a certain intellectual impetus, and till that was spent its administration was supported in a rickety existence by an abnormal strength. But afterwards the Commissioners were left to their intrinsic weakness. There were members for all the localities, but there were none for them. There were members for every crotchet and corrupt interest, but there were none for them. The rural guardians would have liked to eke out wages by rates; the city guardians hated control, and hated to spend money. The Commission had to be dissolved, and a parliamentary head was added; the result is not perfect, but it is an amazing improvement on what would have happened in the old system. The new system has not worked well because the central authority has too little power; but under the previous system the central authority was getting to have, and by this time would have had, no power at all. And if Sir George Lewis and Mr. Chadwick could not maintain an outlying department in the face of Parliament, how unlikely that an inferior compound of discretion and activity will ever maintain it!

These reasonings show why a changing parliamentary head, a head changing as the ministry changes, is a necessity of good Parliamentary government, and there is happily a natural provision that there will be such heads. Party organisation ensures it. In America, where on account of the fixedly recurring presidential election, and the perpetual minor elections, party organisation is much more effectually organised than anywhere else, the effect on the offices is tremendous. Every office is filled anew at every presidential change, at least every change which brings in a new party. Not only the greatest posts, as in England, but the minor posts change their occupants. The scale of the financial operations of the Federal government is now so increased that most likely in that department, at least, there must in future remain a permanent element of great efficiency; a revenue of £90,000,000 sterling cannot be collected and expended with a trifling and changing staff. But till now the Americans have tried to get on not only with changing heads to a bureaucracy, as the English, but without any stable bureaucracy at all. They have facilities for trying it which no one else has. All Americans can administer, and the number of them really fit to be in succession lawyers, financiers, or military managers is wonderful; they need not be as afraid of a change of all their officials as European countries must, for the incoming substitutes are sure to be much better there than here; and they do not fear, as we English fear, that the outgoing officials will be left destitute in middle life, with no hope for the future and no recompense for the past, for in America (whatever may be the cause of it) opportunities are numberless, and a man who is ruined by being "off the rails" in England soon there gets on another line. The Americans will probably to some extent modify their past system of total administrative cataclysms, but their very existence in the only competing form of free government should prepare us for and make us patient with the mild transitions of Parliamentary government.

These arguments will, I think, seem conclusive to almost every one; but, at this moment, many people will meet them thus: they will say, "You prove what we do not deny, that this system of periodical change is a necessary ingredient in Parliamentary government, but you have not proved what we do deny, that this change is a good thing. Parliamentary government may have that effect, among others, for anything we care: we maintain merely that it is a defect." In answer, I think it may be shown, not, indeed, that this precise change is necessary to a permanently perfect administration, but that some analogous change, some change of the same species, is so.

At this moment, in England, there is a sort of leaning towards bureaucracy — at least among writers and talkers. There is a seizure of partiality to it. The English people do not easily change their rooted notions, but they have many unrooted notions. Any great European event is sure for a moment to excite a sort of twinge of conversion to something or other. Just now, the triumph of the Prussians — the bureaucratic people, as is believed, *par excellence* — has excited a kind of admiration for bureaucracy, which a few years since we should have thought impossible. I do not presume to criticise the Prussian bureaucracy of my own knowledge; it certainly is not a pleasant institution for foreigners to come across, though agreeableness to travellers is but of very second-rate importance. But it is quite certain that the Prussian bureaucracy, though we, for a moment, half admire it at a distance, does not permanently please the most intelligent and liberal

Prussians at home. What are two among the principal aims of the *Fortschritt Partei*—the party of progress—as Mr. Grant Duff, the most accurate and philosophical of our describers, delineates them?

First, "a liberal system, conscientiously carried out in all the details of the administration, with a view to avoiding the scandals now of frequent occurrence, when an obstinate or bigoted official sets at defiance the liberal initiations of the government, trusting to backstairs influence."

Second, "an easy method of bringing to justice guilty officials, who are at present, as in France, in all conflicts with simple citizens like men armed *cap-à-pie* fighting with undefenceless." A system against which the most intelligent native liberals bring, even with colour of reason, such grave objections is a dangerous model for foreign imitation.

The defects of bureaucracy are, indeed, well known. It is a form of government which has been tried often enough in the world, and it is easy to show what, human nature being what it in the long run is, the defects of a bureaucracy must in the long run be.

It is an inevitable defect, that bureaucrats will care more for routine than for results; or, as Burke put it, "that they will think the substance of business not to be much more important than the forms of it." Their whole education and all the habit of their lives make them do so. They are brought young into the particular part of the public service to which they are attached; they are occupied for years in learning its forms — afterwards, for years too, in applying these forms to trifling matters. They are, to use the phrase of an old writer, "but the tailors of business; they cut the clothes, but they do not find the body." Men so trained must come to think the routine of business not a means, but an end— to imagine the elaborate machinery of which they form a part, and from which they derive their dignity, to be a grand and achieved result, not a working and changeable instrument. But in a miscellaneous world there is now one evil and now another. The very means which best helped you yesterday may very likely be those which most impede you to-morrow—you may want to do a different thing to-morrow, and all your accumulation of means for yesterday's work is but an obstacle to the new work. The Prussian military system is the theme of popular wonder now,

yet it sixty years pointed the moral against form. We have all
heard the saying that "Frederic the Great lost the battle of
Jena." It was the system which he had established—a good system for his wants and his times, which, blindly adhered to, and
continued into a different age—put to strive with new competitors,
—brought his country to ruin. The "dead and formal" Prussian
system was then contrasted with the "living" French system—the
sudden outcome of the new explosive democracy. The system
which now exists is the product of the reaction; and the history
of its predecessor is a warning what is future history may be too.
It is not more celebrated for its day than Frederic's for his, and
principle teaches that a bureaucracy, elated by sudden success,
and marvelling at its own merit, is the most unimproving and
shallow of governments.

   Not only does a bureaucracy thus tend to under-government, in
point of quality; it tends to over-government, in point of quantity. The trained official hates the rude, untrained public. He
thinks that they are stupid, ignorant, reckless—that they cannot
tell their own interest—that they should have the leave of the
office before they do anything. Protection is the natural inborn
creed of every official body; free trade is an intrinsic idea, alien
to its notions, and hardly to be assimilated with life; and it is
easy to see how an accomplished critic, used to a free and active
life, could thus describe the official.

   "Every imaginable and real social interest," says Mr. Laing,
"religion, education, law, police, every branch of public or private
business, personal liberty to move from place to place, even from
parish to parish within the same jurisdiction; liberty to engage in
any branch of trade or industry, on a small or large scale; all the
objects, in short, in which body, mind, and capital can be employed in civilised society; were gradually laid hold of for the
employment and support of functionaries, were centralised in
bureaux, were superintended, licensed, inspected, reported upon,
and interfered with by a host of officials scattered over the land,
and maintained at the public expense, yet with no conceivable utility
in their duties. They are not, however, gentlemen at large, enjoy-
ing salary without service. They are under a semi-military discipline. In Bavaria, for instance, the superior civil functionary can
place his inferior functionary under house-arrest for neglect of duty,
or other offence against civil functionary discipline. In Wurtemberg,

the functionary cannot marry without leave from his superior. Voltaire says, somewhere, that, 'the art of government is to make two-thirds of a nation pay all it possibly can pay for the benefit of the other third.' This is realised in Germany by the functionary system. The functionaries are not there for the benefit of the people, but the people for the benefit of the functionaries. All this machinery of functionarism, with its numerous ranks and gradations in every district, filled with a staff of clerks and expectants in every department looking for employment, appointments, or promotions, was intended to be a new support of the throne in the new social state of the Continent; a third class, in connection with the people by their various official duties of interference in all public or private affairs, yet attached by their interests to the kingly power. The *Beamptenstand*, or functionary class, was to be the equivalent to the class of nobility, gentry, capitalists, and men of larger landed property than the peasant-proprietors, and was to make up in numbers for the want of individual weight and influence. In France, at the expulsion of Louis Philippe, the civil functionaries were stated to amount to 807,030 individuals. This civil army was more than double of the military. In Germany, this class is necessarily more numerous in proportion to the population, the landwehr system imposing many more restrictions than the conscription on the free action of the people, and requiring more officials to manage it, and the semi-feudal jurisdictions and forms of law requiring much more writing and intricate forms of procedure before the courts than the Code Napoleon."

A bureaucracy is sure to think that its duty is to augment official power, official business, or official members, rather than to leave free the energies of mankind ; it overdoes the quantity of government, as well as impairs its quality.

The truth is, that a skilled bureaucracy—a bureaucracy trained from early life to its special avocation—is, though it boasts of an appearance of science, quite inconsistent with the true principles of the art of business. That art has not yet been condensed into precepts, but a great many experiments have been made, and a vast floating vapour of knowledge floats through society. One of the most sure principles is, that success depends on a due mixture of special and nonspecial minds — of minds which attend to the means, and of minds which attend to the end.

The success of the great joint-stock banks of London — the most remarkable achievement of recent business—has been an example of the use of this mixture. These banks are managed by a board of persons mostly *not* trained to the business, supplemented by, and annexed to, a body of specially trained officers, who have been bred to banking all their lives. These mixed banks have quite beaten the old banks, composed exclusively of pure bankers ; it is found that the board of directors has greater and more flexible knowledge—more insight into the wants of a commercial community—knows when to lend and when not to lend, better than the old bankers, who had never looked at life, except out of the bank windows. Just so the most successful railways in Europe have been conducted—not by engineers or traffic managers—but by capitalists ; by men of a certain business culture, if of no other. These capitalists buy and use the services of skilled managers, as the unlearned attorney buys and uses the services of the skilled barrister, and manage far better than any of the different sorts of special men under them. They combine these different specialties—make it clear where the realm of one ends and that of the other begins, and add to it a wide knowledge of large affairs, which no special man can have, and which is only gained by diversified action. But this utility of leading minds used to generalise, and acting upon various materials, is entirely dependent upon their position. They must not be at the bottom—they must not even be half way up—they must be at the top. A merchant's clerk would be a child at a bank counter ; but the merchant himself could, very likely, give good, clear. and useful advice in a bank court. The merchant's clerk would be equally at sea in a railway office, but the merchant himself could give good advice, very likely, at a board of directors. The summits (if I may so say) of the various kinds of business are, like the tops of mountains, much more alike than the parts below—the bare principles are much the same ; it is only the rich variegated details of the lower strata that so contrast with one another. But it needs travelling to know that the summits *are* the same. Those who live on one mountain believe that *their* mountain is wholly unlike all others.

  The application of this principle to Parliamentary government is very plain ; it shows at once that the intrusion from without upon an office of an exterior head of the office, is not an evil, but that, on the contrary, it is essential to the perfection of that office. If it is left to itself, the office will become technical, self-absorbed, self-multiplying. It will be likely to overlook the end in the means ; it will fail from narrowness of mind ; it will be eager in seeming to do ; it will be idle in real doing. An extrinsic chief is the fit corrector of such errors. He can say to the permanent chief, skilled in the forms and pompous with the memories of his office, "Will you, Sir, explain to me how this regulation conduces to the end in view ? According to the natural view of things, the applicant should state the whole of his wishes to one clerk on one paper ; you make him say it to five clerks on five papers." Or, again, "Does it not appear to you, Sir, that the reason of this formality is extinct. When we were building wood ships, it was quite right to have such precautions against fire ; but now that we are building iron ships," &c., &c. If a junior clerk asked these questions, he would be "pooh-poohed !" It is only the head of an office that can get them answered. It is he, and he only, that brings the rubbish of office to the burning glass of sense.

The immense importance of such a fresh mind is greatest in a country where business changes most. A dead, inactive, agricultural country may be governed by an unalterable bureau for years and years, and no harm come of it. If a wise man arranged the bureau rightly in the beginning, it may run rightly a long time. But, if the country be a progressive, eager, changing one, soon the bureau will either cramp improvement, or be destroyed itself.

This conception of the use of a Parliamentary head shows how wrong is the obvious notion which regards him as the principal administrator of his office. The late Sir George Lewis used to be fond of explaining this subject. He had every means of knowing. He was bred in the permanent civil service. He was a very successful Chancellor of the Exchequer, a very successful Home Secretary, and he died Minister for War. He used to say, "It is not the business of a Cabinet Minister to work his department. His business is to see that it is properly worked. If he does much, he is probably doing harm. The permanent staff of the office can do what he chooses to do much better, or if they cannot, they ought to be removed. He is only a bird of passage, and cannot compete with those who are in the office all their lives round." Sir George Lewis was a perfect Parliamentary head of an office, so far as that head is to be a keen critic and rational corrector of it.

But Sir George Lewis was not perfect; he was not even an average good head in another respect. The use of a fresh mind applied to the official mind is not only a corrective use, it is also an animating use. A public department is very apt to be dead to what is wanting for a great occasion till the occasion is past. The vague public mind will appreciate some signal duty before the precise, occupied administration perceives it. The Duke of Newcastle was of this use at least in the Crimean war. He roused up his department, though when roused it could not act. A perfect Parliamentary minister would be one who should add the animating capacity of the Duke of Newcastle to the accumulated sense, the detective instinct, and the *laissez faire* habit of Sir George Lewis.

As soon as we take the true view of Parliamentary office we shall perceive that, fairly, frequent change in the official is an advantage, not a mistake. If his function is to bring a representative of outside sense and outside animation in contact with the inside world, he ought often to be changed. No man is a perfect representative of outside sense. "There is some one," says the true French saying, "who is more able than Talleyrand, more able than Napoleon. *C'est tout le monde.*" That many-sided sense finds no microcosm in any single individual. Still less are the critical function and the animating function of a Parliamentary minister likely to be perfectly exercised by one and the same man. Impelling power and restraining wisdom are as opposite as any two things, and are rarely found together. And even if the natural mind of the Parliamentary minister was perfect, long contact with the office would destroy his use. Inevitably he would accept the ways of office, think its thoughts, live its life. The "dyer's hand would be subdued to what it works in." If the function of a Parliamentary minister is to be an outsider to his office, we must not choose one who, by habit, thought, and life, is acclimatised to its ways.

There is every reason to expect that a Parliamentary statesman will be a man of quite sufficient intelligence, quite enough various knowledge, quite enough miscellaneous experience, to represent effectually general sense in opposition to bureaucratic sense. Most Cabinet ministers in charge of considerable departments are men of superior ability; I have heard an eminent living statesman of long experience say that in his time he only knew one instance to the contrary. And there is the best protection that it shall be so. A considerable Cabinet minister has to defend his Department in the face of mankind; and though distant observers and sharp writers may depreciate it, this is a very difficult thing. A fool, who has publicly to explain great affairs, who has publicly to answer detective questions, who has publicly to argue against able and quick opponents, must soon be shown to be a fool. The very nature of Parliamentary government answers for the discovery of substantial incompetence.

VIII.

THE CONDUCT OF BUSINESS IN CONGRESS.

[FROM AN ARTICLE BY SENATOR HOAR IN THE NORTH AMERICAN REVIEW, FEB., 1879.]

There are few subjects of equal public interest concerning which so much misunderstanding prevails among well-informed people as the course of business in the national House of Representatives. Most persons think that their representative can at any time, if he choose, rise in his place and demand the attention of the House to a speech on any subject which may interest him or his constituents, and compel the body to record its opinion on any bill or resolution he sees fit to introduce. This is far from being true. The House of Representatives is governed by a complicated and artificial system of rules, so difficult to be understood that many able men of great national fame go through long terms of service without professing to comprehend it. It is not my purpose to write a treatise on this complex arrangement. I wish only to call attention to the operation of a few parts of the mechanism which seem to me to require alteration, and to show how they tend to diminish the authority, weight, and dignity of the House, and how they have deprived that illustrious body of the equality with the Senate which the framers of the Constitution contemplated.

The representatives of the large States in the Convention of 1787 contended earnestly for the apportionment of representation among the States in both branches according to numbers. The representatives of the small-States demanded equality of representation in the Senate. This difference seemed for a long time incapable of adjustment, and nearly caused the Convention to break up without accomplishing its purpose. The difficulty was compromised by the appointment of a committee of one from each State, whose report was adopted with some modification. The large States yielded the equality of representation in the Senate, but demanded and secured for the House the sole power of originating bills for raising revenue. The clause as reported was as follows :

All bills for raising or appropriating money, and for fixing the salaries of the officers of the Government of the United States, shall originate in the first branch of the Legislature, and shall not be altered or amended by the second branch ; and no money shall be drawn from the public treasury but in pursuance of appropriations to be originated in the first branch.

In the second branch, each State shall have an equal vote.

The clause as to revenue bills was adopted in this form :

All bills for raising revenue shall originate in the House of Representatives ; but the Senate may propose or concur with amendments, as on other bills.

It will be observed that, while the Convention voted to confine the power of originating bills for raising revenue to the House, it with equal distinctness voted not to extend this prohibition to bills for appropriating money. The system so established differs from the Constitution of England in three essential particulars : In England, no appropriation for a public purpose can be introduced in the House of Commons without a previous request from the Crown ; no money bill can be amended by the Lords ; and the exclusive prerogative of the Commons extends to all bills for raising or appropriating money. So jealous are the Commons of this prerogative, that the Lords rarely attempt to make any but verbal alterations in money bills, in which the sense or intention is not affected ; and, when the Commons accept these, they make special entries on their journals recording the character and object of the amendments, and their reasons for agreeing to them.

There is no historical evidence that anybody in the Convention gave much consideration to the effect of these changes from the English system upon the value of the prerogative. The better opinion was, that the importance of the privilege, as asserted by the English Commons, was very much exaggerated, and that American experience in those States whose constitutions contained a like provision had shown that it was without advantage, and was a fruitful source of wrangling between the two Houses. Mr. Madison said : "I confess I see nothing of concession in it. The originating money bills is no concession on the part of the smaller States, for, if seven States in the second branch should want such a bill, their interest in the first branch will prevail to bring it forward. It is nothing more than a nominal privilege."

This is one of the few subjects upon which General Washington's vote is recorded : " He disapproved, and till now voted against, the exclusive privilege. He gave up his judgment," he said, " because it was not of very material weight with him, and was made an essential point with others, who, if disappointed, might be less content in other points of real weight."

Similar views were expressed by many of the most eminent members. Three of the larger States, to whom this privilege was offered as a concession, by way of equivalent for the equality of the small States in the Senate, voted against it as an independent proposition. Mr. Hallam, in his " Constitutional History," expresses a similar opinion as to the exaggeration by the House of Commons of the importance of their exclusive privilege. If this view was sound when the scheme was to deny all power of amendment to the Senate, it has infinitely greater weight after the power of amendment has been yielded. The pocket of the Englishman is protected against lavish expenditure by the fact that no 'sixpence of his money can be granted for a public purpose that has not first been asked for by the Crown, on the advice of a responsible and accountable minister, and because none of his possessions can be made the subject of tax, excise, or duty, unless the proposal come from his own representative. The assent of the sovereign and the Lords is only needed to give the force of law to what is the gift of the free will of the Commons.

To the system established by our Constitution, widely departing as it did from the methods by which the unwritten constitutional law of England keeps the power of the purse in the hands of her Majesty's faithful Commons, two important additions have been made by construction. It should be stated that, whenever a question has arisen between the two branches in regard to the construction of this clause in the Constitution, the House of Representatives has invariably had its own way. It was said by Mr. Webster, in the Senate, in 1833 : " The constitutional question must be regarded as important, but it was one which could not be settled by the Senate. It was purely a question of privilege, and the decision of it belonged alone to the House."

1. By a practice as old as the Government itself, the constitutional prerogative of the House has been held to apply to all the general appropriation bills.

2. The power of amendment, as on other bills, has not been held, as between the two Houses, to be limited to the subjects embraced in the bill as sent from the House, or to perfecting its spe-

cial arrangements.   Each House has a rule, which seldom is an
obstacle to the accomplishment of anything which a majority of its
members desire, declaring that no proposition on a subject different from that under consideration shall be admitted under color
of amendment. It seems impossible to doubt that the amendments contemplated by the framers of the Constitution were
amendments touching the particular subject matter to which the
clauses received from the House relate.   The House of Commons,
so strict to assert its prerogative against the Lords, admits the
right of the Lords to amend, by admitting altogether provisions
which are not germane to the other provisions of the bill (189
Hansard, third series, 411).

The rules of our House are so construed that, on the great
appropriation bills, any amendment designed to carry into effect
existing law, or provide for administering any department of the
Government, is held admissible ; and they are never invoked by
the House against the Senate.

If this were all — if the House and Senate were two bodies of
equal numbers, acting under the same rules, and made up substantially of men of the same sort — it is difficult to perceive the
slightest advantage that the House or the people could derive from
this prerogative, so far as it relates to the appropriation of public
money.   The eleven general appropriation bills, and one or more
deficiency bills, are reported annually.   The former are required
by a rule of the House to be reported from the Committee on Appropriations within thirty days after its appointment.   This rule
is seldom obeyed.   These bills contain, on an average, appropriations to the amount of more than two hundred millions, to which
the Senate commonly adds many millions more.   These Senate
amendments embrace every variety of expenditure for the public service, and every variety of new legislation ; the discretion of the upper branch being, in this particular, as absolutely
unaffected by this constitutional barrier as if it had no existence
whatever.   The wishes of the Senate, in case of difference of
opinion in regard to a proposition which the Senate originates,
are much more likely to prevail when that proposition is added to
a measure the House has agreed to, than if the same measure
should originate as a separate bill in the Senate, and be sent to
the House by itself for consideration on its own merits.

The surrender of the power of amendment, then, as it has
invariably been construed, was the surrender of the whole privi-

lege. It has not only destroyed the advantage intended to be
secured for the immediate representatives of the people, but has
given the Senate a considerable preponderance of influence in
legislation. It has enabled the Senate to exert the power of
tacking clauses to bills of supply, and thereby to extort the consent of the House. This power has been always denied in
Parliament, even to the Commons as against the Lords. On
December 9, 1702, it was ordered and declared by the Lords,
" that the annexing any clause or clauses to a bill of aid or
supply, the matter of which is foreign to or different from the matter of the said bill of aid or supply, is unparliamentary, and tends
to the destruction of the Constitution of this Government" (see
Sir Thomas Erskine May's " Parliamentary Practice," seventh
edition, pages 581–583).

But the destruction of the rightful power of the House over
the great appropriation bills which regulate and supply the Government in all its ordinary administrative functions, and which
contain a very large portion of its general legislation, is rendered
more complete by the method of doing business to which the
House has confined itself by its own rules. All appropriation
bills which are first reported in the House must, by their
rules, be first discussed in Committee of the Whole. No bill can
be reported from this committee to the House until every member
has had an opportunity to move as many amendments as he
chooses. Debate cannot be stopped by the previous question.
The House before going into committee may, it is true, order
debate to close on any particular section or on the whole bill at a
fixed time. Yet this does not prevent amendments, and is rarely
resorted to until debate has strayed from the particular subject of
the bill into general political discussion. So far, therefore, as the
consideration of the appropriation bills as originally reported is
concerned, the usages of the House preserve for itself the character of a deliberative assembly, and for each of its members the
privilege of expressing his opinion in debate, and of bringing to
a vote whatever measure he may desire. But these bills then go to
the Senate. They are there examined by the appropriate
committee, and reported to the Senate, where days are spent in
their consideration, with unlimited opportunity for debate and
amendment. Not only is the original bill remodeled, reviewed,
revised, at the pleasure of the Senate, but hundreds of entirely

new provisions are added at the pleasure of the upper branch. The measure which came from the House, the prerogative of originating which is specially secured by the Constitution and guarded by the House with such jealous care, has precisely the same position and weight, neither more nor less, as any proposition moved by a single member of the Senate.

When the bill goes back to the House, containing the Senate amendments, the session is usually far advanced. In the year of the short session the constitutional limit of the life of the House is approaching. In the alternate years, when the session extends into summer, the scorching heats render men eager to leave Washington, and the two branches have usually fixed the time of adjournment by concurrent vote. There is no time for examination, debate, or reference to Committee of the Whole. The House non-concurs in the Senate amendments in the lump, without hearing them read. The Senate insists. A conference is asked and granted. Conference committees are appointed, consisting of three members from each branch, usually the chairman of the Committee on Appropriations, with that member of the committee most conversant with the subject of the bill, and one member of the minority. These committees confer and agree upon a report compromising and compounding all matters of difference between the two Houses as they may be able. Their report is matter of the highest privilege. It may be made at any time, no matter in what business the House be engaged. A member who is speaking may be taken off his feet by its superior claim to attention. No motion to lay it on the table, to indefinitely postpone, or to amend it is in order. The House or Senate must accept it as a whole or reject it as a whole. If it be rejected, a new conference may be ordered, but the result of a conference must sooner or later be accepted in a mass, or the whole bill be lost. The House is all this time under a sort of duress. If it suffer the appropriation bill to fail, the Government must stop, or an extra session be held at midsummer, with its cost and discomfort. Every other year the House votes on the appropriation bill with the knowledge that if it do not agree to amendments on which the Senate insists, and the bill fail, its power over the subject must be lost altogether by the arrival of the 4th of March, when its life expires, and the new bill must be dealt with by its successors.

Degrading as this system is to the House as a body, its effect on the individual member is still more remarkable. The whole

power of legislation over that vast field which is covered by the
Senate's amendments to the great appropriation bills is in practice
delegated to two of the three members who are appointed on the
conference committee. No other member gets a chance to discuss
them, to vote separately on any one of them, to make any motion
in relation to them, or even to see in print what the committee
recommend in regard to them. " Gape, sinner, and swallow."

If the reader has followed this somewhat technical statement,
he has observed that while the power of amendment reserved in
our Constitution, as it is expounded in practice, allows to the
Senate and to each of its members the fullest opportunity to deal
with appropriation and revenue bills as freely as with bills relating
to any other subject, the rules and usages of the House leave that
body with much less practical power of deliberation or amendment
in regard to all those provisions which have their origin in the
Senate than the House of Lords has in relation to money bills
under the English system.

Suppose, now, all this were reversed. Suppose the Constitution
were to provide that all money bills should originate in the Senate,
permitting the House to amend, as in the case of other bills. The
House would then, on the arrival of the bill, commit it to the
Committee of the Whole, where every clause proposed by the
Senate and every amendment proposed in the House would be
fully discussed, with unlimited power to propose changes, every
individual member having the fullest opportunity to express his
opinion or offer his plan ; and the conference committee of both
branches would receive the bill fully possessed of the views of
their respective Houses as to every syllable which had been proposed by either. When, therefore, the large States accepted the
clause in question as a partial equivalent for the equality of the
small States in the Senate, they accepted a further limitation of
their own power. When the House, in 1832, refused to permit
Mr. Clay's compromise bill to have its origin in the Senate ; when,
in 1856, it refused to permit the Senate to originate some of the
general appropriation bills ; and when, in 1870, it refused to
permit the Senate to add a revision of the whole tariff to a bill
abolishing the duties on tea and coffee, its victory was an abdica-
tion of its equality in legislation with the Senate, and tended to
deprive every one of its members of his right to debate or amendment in regard to a large part of the most important legislation of
the country.

I have been speaking of the course of the ordinary business of Congress. Upon the great questions which move the heart of the nation and divide political parties, the body of the House and its leaders are commonly in full accord, and the representatives of the American people know how to make their power felt and assume their rightful and constitutional place in legislation. But even here it is not enough that the House preserves its power. The power to do what it will, and to refuse consent to what it will not, will not preserve its own dignity or its value as an important factor in legislation, unless its will is the result of its best judgment; in other words, unless it preserve its function as a deliberative assembly. The difficulty is not that on great occasions and great questions the voice of the House is stifled. On such occasions the House and its leaders are in accord with each other, and commonly in accord with a public sentiment which the Senate will not lightly resist. But the practice I have been exposing tends largely to take from the House the character of a deliberative assembly. The barren and empty privilege of originating bills of revenue and bills of supply it has purchased at the sacrifice of that essential prerogative—essential to its own dignity and to that of every individual among its members—its freedom of debate.

Let us pass now from the subject of money bills to a glance at the methods of general legislation. The morning hour of every Monday is devoted by the House to a call of all the States and Territories for the introduction of bills and joint resolutions. The House commonly takes care that every member has full opportunity to introduce as many bills as he desires. These bills are usually printed. The rule is peremptory that they shall be at once referred to their appropriate committees without debate and without the right to move to reconsider the vote of reference. Several thousand bills are introduced in this way in every Congress. Worthy citizens interested in special reforms are much gratified to read that their member has introduced some excellent and radical measures of reform. The bills themselves are copied by approving newspapers, and redound greatly to the credit of their enterprising authors. For all practical purposes, they might as well be published in a newspaper in New Zealand or Alaska. The processes by which these bills are strangled will be understood by comprehending the operation of the committees and the effect of the previous question.

The House has forty-seven permanent committees, and usually half a dozen special committees on important subjects. Appropriation bills, revenue bills, contested-election cases, and resolutions authorizing the necessary public printing may be reported at any time. All other national legislation can only, under the rules, be reported from the appropriate committee when it is called by the Speaker for reports in its turn. For this call, an hour after the reading of the Journal, on every day except Monday and Friday, is set apart. Each committee is entitled, when it is called, to occupy this morning hour of each of two successive days with the measures which it has prepared, and, if its second morning hour expire while the House is actually considering one of its measures, to have that single measure hold over in the morning hour till it is disposed of. Supposing the two sessions which make up the life of the House to last ten months, and allowing for the holidays, the time taken for organization and appointing committees, and the time when the four privileged subjects above named take up the attention of the House, so that the morning hour can not be devoted to this call, I suppose one hundred days in two sessions is an unusually large average of days when such a call is had. This gives an average of not more than two hours apiece to the committees of the House to report upon, debate, and dispose of all the subjects of general legislation committed to their charge. From this time is taken the time consumed in reading the bill, and in calling the yeas and nays, which may be ordered by one-fifth of the members present, and which requires forty minutes for a single roll-call. The members of the committees, of course, take special interest in the subjects assigned to them, which they have investigated and reported, and which they have prepared themselves to discuss. It will readily be believed, therefore, that the House is inclined to shorten rather than to lengthen the time given to any one matter — each member eager that the committee holding the floor shall give way as soon as possible, that the call may go on and his own committee's turn come the sooner. The committee holding the floor, if it have several measures matured, desires to hurry each along as fast as possible, that it may dispose of the others. After the bill is reported, the member reporting it is entitled to the floor for an hour. If the previous question is ordered, he has a further hour to sum up. No amendment can be offered till the member's first hour is over, and none after the previous question is ordered. The result is, that the floor is held by the member who made the report, and parceled out by yielding portions of his time to persons who desire to speak for or against the measure. The sense of fair play in the House usually secures an equal division of the time allowed for debate between friends and foes. But the person who reports the bill dictates how long the debate shall last, who shall speak on each side, and whether any and what amendments shall be offered. Any member fit to be intrusted with the charge of an important measure would be deemed guilty of an inexcusable blunder if he surrendered the floor, which the usages of the House assign to his control for an hour, without demanding the previous question. The House in rare instances refuses to grant the demand, but this is at the hazard of prolonging debate indefinitely, which, for the reason above stated, is usually the last thing which any considerable number of members desire. Another expedient is more frequent. A minority who wish to secure a chance to debate or amend a specially obnoxious bill sometimes bring the majority to terms by what is called filibustering, that is, consuming time by repeated motions to adjourn, on which the yeas and nays are called, so that no progress is made in business until the majority grant time for debate or agree to test the sense of the House by permitting an amendment to be moved. These difficulties, which stand in the way of the introduction of bills in the regular mode under the rules, and beset them after they are introduced, have led to another device by means of which a large proportion, perhaps a majority, of all the bills which pass the House are carried through. Every Monday after the morning hour, and at any time during the last ten days of the session, motions to suspend the rules are in order. At these times any member may move to suspend the rules and pass any proposed bill. It requires two-thirds of the members voting to adopt such motion. Upon it no debate or amendment is in order. In this way, if two-thirds of the body agree, a bill is by a single vote, without discussion and without change, passed through all the necessary stages, and made law so far as the consent of the House can accomplish it ; and in this mode hundreds of measures of vital importance receive, near the close of exhausting sessions, without being debated, amended, printed, or understood, the constitutional assent of the representatives of the American people.

In administering this system, the general outline of which I have given, many subtle and artificial constructions and distinctions have been established, which it is not necessary to deal with here. I have failed to make myself understood if the reader has not seen how completely, by its own rules, the House has deprived itself of "that freedom of deliberation, speech, and debate" which our early American constitutions declare to be " essential to the rights of the people." This result has been brought about by what is called " the previous question " — a guillotine which is in constant operation.

*　　*　　*　　*　　*　　*　　*　　*　　*

The Senate, on its first organization in 1789, adopted by its rules the previous question as used in the House of Commons. On the 17th of March, 1806, it established a new code of rules in which no mention is made of the previous question ; but the eighth rule was as follows :

While a question is before the Senate, no motion shall be received, unless for an amendment, for postponing the question, or to commit it, or to adjourn ; and the motion for adjournment shall always be in order, and shall be decided without debate.

By this rule the Senate abolished the previous question altogether. For seventy-two years there has been no restraint in that body upon the liberty of debate and the power of amendment. Mr. Foot of Connecticut proposed, on the 23d of January, 1832, that the question of consideration should be decided without debate. This was denounced by Mr. Benton as an invasion of the liberty of speech, and was not pressed.

In 1841, after twelve years of Democratic rule, the Whigs took possession of the Government, with a majority of nearly fifty in the House and of seven in the Senate. On the 6th day of July, at the extra session, the rules of the House were amended by adding that the House might, "by a majority vote, provide for the discharge of the Committee" (of the Whole) "from the consideration of any bill referred to them, after acting without debate upon all amendments pending and that may be offered." This was carried by a vote of 117 to 95, after a considerable struggle. John Quincy Adams speaks of it in his diary as "a new screw."

*　　*　　*　　*　　*　　*　　*　　*　　*

Immediately after the declaration of the vote, Mr. Lott Warren of Georgia, with a view, as he said, "to carry out the reform which had been begun," announced his purpose to offer as an amendment to the twenty-eighth rule : "And that no member be

allowed to speak more than one hour to any question under debate."
This was adopted on the following day, June 7th; yeas 111, nays
75. Mr. Adams records in his diary: "I voted against the resolution, but hope it will effect much good." On the 8th of June,
the House being in committee on the loan bill, while Mr. Pickens
was speaking in opposition, the Chair reminded him that his hour
was out. Mr. Pickens denied that the House had any constitutional right to pass such a rule. The Chair again reminded Mr.
Pickens that he had spoken an hour. Mr. Pickens would then conclude by saying that it was the most infamous rule ever passed
by any legislative body.

With this ineffective remonstrance the minority of the House
submitted to the inauguration of the practice, which has ever since
prevailed with constantly increasing strictness. I suppose the large
majority of measures which pass the House of Representatives are
passed on motion to suspend the rules and adopt the bill, on which
motion neither debate nor amendment is permitted, or under the
previous question, moved by the member who introduces the measure at the time of its introduction, either wholly without discussion
or amendment, or with only so much of either as the mover, in his
discretion, sees fit to allow.

* * * * * * * * *

One other peculiarity of the conduct of business in the House,
under its present methods, is the absence of responsible leadership. In the British Parliament, the whole executive power of the
Government is lodged. The prime minister, if a commoner, is the
recognized leader of the majority of the House of Commons; if
he is a peer, the function of leadership of that House is vested in a
member of the Government, selected for that purpose usually for
his tact and ability in debate. Differences of opinion, jealousies,
struggles for personal advancement, distract the counsels of political parties in England as they do with us; but they are
reserved for the secrecy of cabinet discussions, and are not
permitted to show themselves in public in the House.

Lord Palmerston's diary for May 22, 1828, gives a curious account of the conduct of business in the cabinet. of which he was
a member:

The cabinet has gone on for some time past as it had done before, differing upon almost every question of any importance that
has been brought under consideration; meeting to debate and dispute, and separating without deciding.

To this Sir Henry Bulwer adds :

I can not help observing, with reference to the sentence last quoted, that the father of the late Lord Holland, who had lived almost all his life with cabinet ministers, once said to me that he had never known a cabinet in which its members did not dispute more among themselves during their councils than they disputed with their antagonists in the House of Commons.

These discords disappear when the measures of the Government are brought into the publicity of the House of Commons. Her Majesty's Government are responsible for the due preparation of all important measures. By the standing orders the right is reserved to her Majesty's ministers of placing Government orders at the head of the list on every order day except Wednesday ; and near the close of the session this precedence is extended to other days, and sometimes to Wednesdays. In our House the business suffers from the want of some such arrangement. All subjects of legislation are parceled out among the different committees. Each of these almost comes to regard itself as a little legislature, and contends with great jealousy against encroachments on its own jurisdiction.

With rare and conspicuous exceptions of persons who bring to the House when they enter it a reputation which insures them a place at the head of some important committee, the members attain places of influence on these committees by seniority. The House becomes in this way a sort of presbytery, the senior member of each leading committee having special influence over his own subject. The result is, that there is a struggle between the different leading committees for the opportunity to bring their questions before the House. Toward the close of the session this contest becomes specially apparent. A member who has carefully prepared some important measure, with which he is identified in public estimation, feels that the success or failure of his political career depends upon his getting an opportunity to bring it to a vote. As the termination of the session approaches, the appropriation bills press for passage. The rules of the House give the Committees on Appropriations and on Ways and Means, who have charge of the kindred measures of revenue, the right to report at any time when a member is not speaking. The right to report from a conference committee is even more highly privileged, and may be exercised when a member is actually on his feet in the midst of a speech. The chairman of the Committee on Appropriations, who may be held responsible if one of the great bills under his charge fails, and an extra session is made necessary, feels that he must use his power without much mercy. The result is, that he becomes almost the natural enemy of every other important bill before the House.

*   *   *   *   *   *   *   *   *

It would be easy to multiply instances. The strength of the personal influence of able and popular men is and must be very great in a body composed as is our House of Representatives. But there is no man on the floor whose position gives him the right to lead ; no man who is responsible that each measure receives its due share of attention ; no man of prominence who is not likely to have matters under his special charge which, in the struggle for the command of the previous hours when the session draws near its end, tempt him to thrust out of the House other measures of equal public consequence.

It is needless to set forth at length the evils which this state of things brings forth. There is one which I regard as peculiarly unfortunate for the character and dignity of the House, and whose bad consequences can hardly be overstated. It is that almost inevitably the Speaker of the House is forced into the position of a party leader.

The space of this article will not allow me to point out other kindred evils that have grown up in the recent practice of the House of Representatives. Those to which I have called attention are the most important, and are growing year by year. The House is losing its freedom of debate, of amendment, even of knowledge of what it is itself doing. A member is almost the last person to ask what is contained in an appropriation bill on its final passage. More and more the contest over important measures is a contest, not whether they shall be discussed, but whether they shall be brought to a vote. The Speaker becomes a party leader, while obliged to observe forms of impartiality. There is nowhere responsibility for securing due attention to important measures, and no authority to decide between their different claims.

The chairman of the principal committee becomes almost the natural enemy of every other committee in the House.

I must take another occasion to deal with the question of remedy for these evils. I do not believe in radical changes in the

122 CONDUCT OF BUSINESS IN CONGRESS.

institutions of the state, contrived by *doctrinaires*. The practice of the House of Representatives is a growth, not a scheme. Still less would I urge a blind reverence for English examples. But if we could in some way secure a Speaker who should be absolutely independent of party it would be a great gain. If the three committees, Ways and Means, Appropriations, Banking and Currency, could be blended in one, as formerly, the number of this committee to be at least fifteen, dividing its functions among sub-commitees, the chairman never himself to have charge of an Appropriation bill, but to be responsible for the order of business of the House, subject, of course, to the control of the body itself, a great step in efficiency would be gained.

But the great point, the restoration to the House of its function of a deliberative assembly, can only be fully accomplished by a reduction of its members. I know the strong objections to this reduction. For obvious reasons, it is not likely to receive the assent of the House itself, until demanded by an irresistible public opinion. That demand may be long delayed, perhaps avoided altogether, by making provision for removing from Congress the consideration of private claims, thereby diminishing the pressure of business, and by a reorganization of the system of committees, which shall give the House the benefit of responsible leadership.

IX

THE HOUSE OF REPRESENTATIVES.

[FROM "THE NATION," APRIL 4, 1878.]

ALTHOUGH the galleries of the House are daily crowded, very few of the American people have a clear idea of the conditions under which work is done there. A vague opinion is prevalent that a member of Congress can take the floor when he pleases, move any resolution or bill he has a mind to, and make an hour's speech on any subject he fancies his constituents in Buncombe County may want discussed. A reading of the *Congressional Record* or the Associated Press despatches is quite as likely to confirm as to weaken this opinion ; for in the varied phenomena that are presented it would need a Darwin or a Huxley so to co-ordinate them as to find any governing rule or law, or even to guess at the system on which the phantasmagoria is constructed. Yet there is a system and a law, or rather a code of laws, known as the Rules of the House, complex and voluminous, the long and patient study of which, joined to patient and persevering practice, is absolutely necessary if a Representative has any ambition to become a "good parliamentarian," or would hope to conduct an important measure to a successful conclusion.

Many a new member, with a budget of bills and resolutions which he fondly believes are destined to reveal to the country its future great statesman, has entered the Hall of the House in undoubting faith that he has passed the portals of a brilliant career. He rises in his place and addresses the Chair. He is sure he was up as quickly as any one, but the Speaker seems unaware of his existence. He is a little dazed by the fact that a dozen more are doing the same thing, and that the loud talking, the clapping of hands for the pages, and the total unconsciousness of the body that he is trying to gain an audience, make a combination of untoward circumstances very like trying to address the people in the omnibuses from the curbstone in front of the Astor House, and he takes his seat a little flustered, thinking he will watch the course of things a little and try it again. The

next time he determines that he will not be foiled by modesty, and
shouts "Mr. Speaker" so loudly that, as much to be rid of him as
for anything else, he is recognized by the Chair. "I desire to
present a resolution and ask its adoption." "It can only be done
at this time by unanimous consent," the Speaker replies, and
"I object" is heard from several members at once. Some one
else is given the floor, and our friend subsides again to reflect
upon the cruel obstacles in his path of glory. By the help of
diligent thumbing of the Rules, and by curbing his pride so as to
seek some advice of an old member, he learns that the Roll of
the States will be called on Monday and then he will be in order.
He plucks up fresh courage and on that day is on the alert, his
State is called, he gets the floor, sends his resolution to the clerk
and clears his throat for a speech. A sharp rap of the gavel is
followed by "No debate is in order; the resolution can only be
referred to the proper Committee," and before he can rightly
understand what has happened the current has swept by him, and
he takes his seat with a waning sense of his own importance.
But he will not give it up so. He finds what committee has
charge of his precious resolution, and tries to impress its chairman with the importance of his measure. "Bless you," he is told,
"there are fifty on the same subject; they will go to a sub-com-
mittee, and by and by we may report something. Wait and see."
He waits, and a month or more afterward he some morning
catches a few words of a report from that committee, which imply
that they have introduced a bill which is ordered to be printed
and recommitted. He gets a copy of the bill, finds it at war with
all his ideas, and burns with the thought of exposing its folly and
vindicating the wisdom and policy of his own proposition. Now,
at least, he will be in order and shall be heard. Still there are
delays, but a day is set for discussion, and he is fully prepared.
One speaker after another is recognized, but he fails to get the
floor. His shouts to the Speaker are unnoticed; he becomes
angry and flurried. Some one asks him if he has any arrangement with the committee or with the Speaker for time to speak.
No, he answers; but has he not the right to be heard? No;
debate is almost always limited to the members of the committee
having the measure in charge and a few whom they may favor
with the opportunity to speak. His wish to be heard at last over-
comes his pride and wrath, and he is introduced to some member

of the committee, who is good-humored enough (exceptionally good humored) to yield the new man a few minutes of his time. And so he gets a tithe of the time he wanted to develop his subject, and under nervous condition, which forbid thought, amid surroundings to the last degree discouraging, he says a few words without pleasure to himself or profit to the House, and resumes his chair full of inward objurgations at a system which seems ingeniously contrived to prevent the satisfactory discussion of public business, and to give exclusive control of what is done to the Speaker and the older members of the majority who are chairmen of the important committees.

His own committee-work is probably quite as disgusting to him. He may have come to the House brimful of revenue reform, and find himself assigned as "end man" to the Committee on Expenditures in the Department of Justice, with nothing to do. He may have been a leading jurist of mature experience, but unless he has the touchstone of long service in the House he may wish in vain for a place on the Judiciary Committee; he is buried in the Committee on Manufactures, which has but one meeting and never a report in a long session. If he is a member of the majority and has had some political prominence outside, his case is a better one, and some chance for important work may be given him; but even this may prove a delusion and a snare, as Mr. Ewing found to his cost at the present session, when his lack of knowledge of the rules gave his opponents an instant advantage of him, and put his resumption-repeal "in the nine holes," from which he could not take it till he yielded the terms of debate which were demanded, and surrendered all the expected *éclat* of a prompt passage of his bill under suspension of the rules. His experience only deepened the conviction of all the leading men of the House, that it is folly to trust the floor-management of any important measure to any other than an old hand. Compliments to prominent politicians who are new members must be given in some other way.

The truth is that the rules and customs of the House are the result of a natural selection which, however we may scold at it, was the best the circumstances permitted. The practice may be modified or pruned a little, but no great change can be made till the circumstances are changed. The things most frequently and most justly complained of are the almost despotic power of the

Speaker, the absorption of the lead in business by the older members of a few committees, and the absence of that kind of business debate which should characterize a really deliberating body. Let us look a little at each of these.

The power of the Speaker results from the functions directly committed to him. He appoints the committees. The Senate may elect them, but the House is too large a body for that. The log-rolling combinations that would come of an attempt at election would disgust the nation, and would render the organization of the House an almost endless task. The delay alone would be unendurable. But the appointment of the committees implies the distribution of work to every member. It means the determination of the cast business shall take. It decides for or against all large matters of policy, or may so decide: for, while Speakers will differ one another greatly in force of character and in 'the wish to give positive direction to affairs, the weakest man cannot escape from the necessity of arranging the appointments with a view to the probable character of measures which will be agitated. This, however, is far from the measure of the Speaker's power. All rules are more or less flexible. The current of precedents is never consistent or uniform. The bias of the Speaker at a critical point will turn the scale. Mr. Randall as Speaker determined the assent of the House to the action of the Electoral Commission. Had he wished for a revolutionary attempt to prevent the announcement of Hayes's election, no one who has had experience in Congress, at least, will doubt that he could have forced the collision.

The Speaker's power to award the floor to those whom he may choose to recognize is an enormous one. There are general rules which every Speaker will profess to follow, but they are vague and give abundant latitude. The necessity of getting on with business has given birth to the practice of recognizing the chairmen of leading committees, or those in charge of important pending measures, in preference to other members. The nominal rule is that the man first addressing the chair has the right to the floor, but the rule is only nominal. It is so evident that business could not get on in that way that a member would only be laughed at for trying to insist upon it. Again, it is very rarely the case that several persons are not trying to get the floor at once, and no one but the Speaker could decide among them. An appeal from his decision therefore would be futile. The custom has naturally grown out of this to arrange with the Speaker beforehand for recognition. A member will speak to him privately and in advance, saying, I have such and such a measure to introduce, and I want to be recognized when I rise. A fair-minded Speaker will only enquire far enough to see that the matter is legitimate and important; but if he is unscrupulous it is easy to see how far his power may go. Rumor has it that when Mr. Blaine was Speaker it was hard to get the floor unless the thing to be urged pleased him, and it is even hinted that he required amendments to be made to resolutions, etc., before he would permit them to be offered. Whether this is true or not, it is easy to see that a vigorous, domineering man could easily make it true with such power in his hands. The only real check upon the Speaker must be the public sentiment of the House, and the older members are the natural exponents and voices of this. The minority can do little to check him until his acts become so arrogant and partial as to shock the moderate men of the majority. The leading men of the dominant party are always those whom the Speaker has assigned to important chairmanships of committees, and they are prevented by delicacy and a sense of obligation from opposing him if it can be avoided. A disappointed man will be sure to have his hostility to the Chair attributed to his failure to get an important place, and he will get little sympathy. There is, therefore, small chance for controlling the power of the presiding officer until he goes beyond all endurable bounds, and this a man of any prudence and ability will rarely do. The power of the Speaker of the House over legislation may not unfairly be reckoned much larger than that of the President, and scarcely less than that of the Senate. To this we have come by the slow growth of a hundred years, accelerating, however, as the numbers of the members of the House have increased.

The power of the chairmen of committees follows as a sort of corollary from that of the Speaker. Their leading influence elects him, his favor appoints them, and the latter, with the aid of the exigencies of public business, gives them the practical control of the floor. By custom the chairman of a committee appoints, or at least nominates, its clerk, and he has the lion's share of the clerk's labor and assistance. He has, therefore, better facilities for informing himself as to business before them. He distributes the work to sub-committees, and if he be at all able and politic will practically control the reports and the presentation of all business from his committee to the House. He will usually decide who shall speak on a measure, how long the debate shall continue, when the previous question shall be called, and how the hour of debate which follows the ordering of the previous question shall be apportioned. If any one protests, the ready answer is, How else, in such a Babel, can business make progress at all? Some one must be trusted to direct it, and who so fit, under the superior power of the Speaker, as the chairman of the committee which had a measure in charge and is presumed to have matured it?

Out of these conditions it would be hard, at best, to bring satisfactory and business-like debate. In the English House of Commons the Speaker is a professional moderator, non-partisan, judicial, holding his office sometimes during nearly a lifetime, through all changes of party. The party leaders on the floor control the presentation and debate of measures, and have the rules applied for them by an experienced man acting with a sense of responsibility like that of a judge. Under such a system, aided by a better set of physical surroundings, of which we shall speak presently, it is for the interest of party leaders that they shall bring out the available talent on their side, and in practice the impatience of the House of Commons with a tedious speaker or one talking only "for buncombe" is a sufficient gag-rule. With us, however, impatience rarely takes the active, aggressive form of coughing or scraping a speaker down. If a member of the House of Representatives does not choose to listen, he has his desk, his writing material, his file of letters to answer, his own speech to prepare, and works away careless whether the day is used up in one way or another, until he begins to fear that he shall not get away from the capital before the dog-days. Even then he is more likely to go and scold privately at the chairman of the Committee on Appropriations for not hurrying bills along faster, than to interrupt or try to silence the talker on the floor. It is in this way that the habit of inattention, of noisy side-talk, of utter disregard to the person having the floor, has grown up. It has naturally led also to the custom of writing out speeches and reading them. A member is determined to be heard by the country, or at least by his constituents, if the House will not hear him, and he reads on amidst utter confusion, consoling himself that his speech will be in the *Congressional Record*, an abstract of it in the press despatches, and pamphlet copies can be sent to his people at home. To prove that this kills debate needs no argument. The dulness of the reading of essays reacts upon the disposition to inattention, and the noise and confusion increase the disposition to write rather than to try to speak, and so the evil perpetuates itself, getting larger as it goes. From it comes, too, the custom of getting leave to print speeches not delivered. Why should the House remain to go through the form of pretending to be addressed by a reader who is not heard? Somebody will exclaim, "O print, print!" and the unhappy essayist will be glad to take the hint and ask the requisite permission. There are times, of course, when this is not improper or objectionable, as when an important measure is passing almost without time for debate, whilst members feel unwilling to let their votes go upon record wholly unexplained, or to be regarded as responsible for the motives or arguments that the press may attribute to them.

Even when a man would fain take part in earnest, business-like speech, the physical conditions about him are such as are almost insurmountable. First, the hall of the House is itself so large that few men have voice enough to fill it, even if quiet prevailed on the floor.* If every member must have his desk, and the hall must be surrounded on all sides by deep galleries, no less a room would answer; and by the same token, as we increase the number of members, the Coliseum itself would soon be none too large. But the noise of the House is simply overpowering. In so large a room the loud conversation of disorderly members does not reach the ear distinctly, but the multiplicity of such sounds, added to the manifold forms of noise which the inattentive habits of the body beget, combine into a loud, murmurous roar. which makes one who is beginning to speak feel as if his voice were lost in a tempest or in the noise of surf upon the shore. He instinctively tries to rise his tones above it, and to catch attention by extraordinary effort to be loud. He is shouting before he knows it, and vainly struggling to drown a multitudinous sound for which his lungs are no match. Men of fine intellect and of good ordinary elocution have exclaimed in despair that in the House

---

* The hall of the House of Representatives is 139 feet long and 93 feet wide; that of the House of Commons is 60 feet long and 45 feet wide. The H. of R. has less than half as many members as the H. of C.

of Representatives the mere physical effort to be heard uses up all the powers, so that intellectual action becomes impossible. The natural refuge is in the written speeches or in habitual silence which one dreads more and more to break. The exceptions only prove this rule. Passages-at-arms between gladiators of the stump will generally draw around a crowd of amused lookers-on. A special reputation for wit or for ugly hits will secure a hearing. And occasionally the pre-eminent ability of a speech may overcome all obstacles and fasten attention.

Experienced members of Congress commonly agree that the debates in Committee of the Whole under the five-minute rule are the most profitable that occur in the House. The real shaping of measures occurs at this time, and attention is better given, because all members who feel any responsibility for business know that they must watch at such times if they would act intelligently. The short limit of time necessitates an attempt at terseness, the game of "give and take" between speakers is likely to be lively, and something like a real grappling between opponents takes place. This only adds point to what has been said above about the failure of business debate in the House, for the exception does not occur when the House is in regular session, but when it is in committee—that is to say, the Speaker has left the chair, calling some one to act as temporary chairman of the committee; and during this time no vote by yeas and nays can be taken, no business can be considered but the bills in their order on the calender as they have been referred by the House to the committee, and no final action can be taken except to report to the House when it resumes its regular session the recommendations of the Committee of the Whole.

A suggestion has been made by Mr. Hewitt, of New York, which, if adopted, would remedy most of the physical obstacles to debate which have been described, and would soon improve the style of speaking, making the House a far more attractive field for able men. The plan is to divide the hall of the House in two, arrange one-half of it with benches facing each other on the two sides of the House, as is the case in the English House of Commons. This half of the House should be sacred to debate. No business should be done there but the discussion of bills and resolutions and action upon them. Quiet and order should be rigidly enforced. The other half of the hall should be fitted with the present or other similar conveniences for writing, and for conversation and such other business as the members now transact at their desks or in the lobbies. At the doors leading from the one hall to the other should be a gong or bell to notify members when a division was demanded or a vote to be taken. Those who chose to listen would be in the hall with benches ; those who had more important work to do could remain in the outer hall. The attractiveness of the speaker who might be up, or the importance of the subject, would determine the audience in the speaking-hall, and the leaders or chairman of the committee in charge of the special measure would, as now, control the length of the debate. With such a change would come ease of speaking, quieter tone, better thinking on the feet, better taste in oratory, better progress in everything that makes profitable business discussion, and better progress also in the public business. We could wish there were hope that men enough in Congress appreciate the great desirability of these things to make a fair trial of the experiment.

X

RULES OF THE HOUSE OF COMMONS RELATING TO "OBSTRUCTION" AND TO ORDER OF BUSINESS.

46. The time for the Ordinary Meeting of The House (except on Wednesday* or any day appointed for a Morning Sitting) is at a quarter before Four o'clock, unless some other time shall have been agreed upon.

67 A. No motion for the Adjournment of the House shall, be made until all the Questions on the Notice paper have been disposed of, and no such motion shall be made before the Orders of the Day or Notices of Motion have been entered upon, except by leave of the House, unless a member rising in his place shall propose to move the Adjournment for the purpose of discussing a definite matter of urgent public importance, and not less than Forty Members shall thereupon rise in their places to support the motion; or unless, if fewer than Forty Members and not less than ten shall thereupon rise in their places, the House shall, on a division upon a question put forthwith, determine whether such motion shall be made. [1882.]

67 B. When a motion is made for the Adjournment of a debate, or of the House during any debate, or that the Chairman of a Committee do Report Progress or do leave the Chair, the debate thereon shall be confined to the matter of such motion; and no Member having moved or seconded any such motion shall be entitled to move, or second, any similar motion during the same debate. [1882.]

67 C. If Mr. Speaker shall be of opinion that a motion for Adjournment is an abuse of the rules of the House, he may forthwith put the question thereupon. [1882. Applies also in Committee.]

69 A. If at any sitting of the House any Member shall take notice that Strangers are present, Mr. Speaker shall forthwith put

---

* On Wednesday The House meets at 12 o'clock and is adjourned, by Standing Order, at 6 o'clock.

the Question that Strangers be ordered to withdraw, without permitting any Debate or Amendment. [1882. Applies also in Committee.]

82. Any Member present in the House at Prayers, is entitled to secure a place by affixing his name to a seat.

85. A member not having been present at Prayers, is not entitled to retain any seat during his absence ; but he is generally permitted, by courtesy, to secure it by leaving upon it a book, a hat, or a glove.

87. The front bench, on the right hand of the Chair, is reserved for Members holding office under the Crown ; and the front bench on the left hand of the Chair is ordinarily occupied by Privy Councillors and other Members who have held office under the Crown.

98. The House generally proceeds each day with (1) Private Business ; (2) Public Petitions ; (3) Giving Notices of Motions ; (4) Unopposed Motions for Returns ; (5) Motions for leave of Absence ; (6) Questions [addressed to Ministers] ; (7) Orders of the Day and Notice of Motions as set down in the Order Book.

99. Any Member desiring to give Notice of a Motion may enter his name on the Notice Paper placed upon the Table of the House.

100. At the time for giving Notices the precedence of Members is determined by ballot (= lot).

105. [No notice to be given for any day beyond the next four Notice days (= Tuesdays)].

120. A question may be superseded : (1) By the Adjournment of The House, either on the Motion of a Member, "That this House do *now* adjourn," or on notice being taken, and it appearing that Forty Members are not present ; * * * * (3) By the Previous Question, viz., "That this Question be now put" being proposed and negatived ; and (4) By Amendment.

125 A. When it shall appear to Mr. Speaker during any Debate that the subject has been adequately discussed, and that it is the evident sense of The House that the Question be now put, he may so inform The House ; and if a Motion be made "that the Question be now put," Mr. Speaker shall forthwith put such Question ; and if the same be decided in the affirmative, the question under discussion shall be put forthwith : [Provided that the Question, That The Question be now put, shall not be decided in the affirmative, if a Division be taken, unless it shall appear to

have been supported by more than two hundred Members, or unless
it shall appear to have been opposed by less than forty Members, and supported by more than one hundred Members.]   [1882.
This rule applies also in Committee.]

220 A. B. C. and D. [Provide for the appointment of two
Standing Committees of not less than sixty and not more than
eighty Members ; one for the consideration of bills relating to
Law and Courts of Justice and Legal Procedure, the other for bills
relating to Trade, Shipping and Manufactures. The Members to
be nominated by a Committee of the House. All bills reported
from these Committees are to be proceeded with as if reported from
Committee of the whole House.]

———

406. The House will receive no petition for any sum, or proceed upon any motion for a grant or charge upon the Public' Revenue, whether payable out of the Consolidated Fund or out of
money to be provided by Parliment, unless recommended from the
Crown.

425 A. Whenever Committee of Supply stands as the first
Order of the Day on Monday or Thursday, Mr. Speaker shall leave
the Chair without putting any question, unless * * * an Amendment be moved relating to the Estimates proposed to be taken in
Supply. [1882. "Grievance before Supply."]

———

145. A Member is not to read his speech but may refresh his
memory by reference to notes.

148. When two or more members rise to speak, Mr. Speaker
calls upon the Member who first rose in his place.

159. A new Member who has not yet spoken is generally called
upon, by courtesy, in preference to other members rising at the
same time.

———

152 A. Mr Speaker may call the attention of the House to continued irrelevance or tedious repetition on the part of a member ;
and may direct the Member to discontinue his speech. [1882.]

173 A. [1882. Any member "named" for disregarding the
authority of the Chair, or for abusing the rules of the House by
persistently and willfully obstructing business, may be "suspended from the service of the House" ; the first suspension to be
for a week, the second for a fortnight, and later ones for a
month.]

XI

JURISDICTION OF UNITED STATES' COURTS AND OF STATE COURTS.

[FROM COOLEY'S CONSTITUTIONAL LAW IN THE UNITED STATES:
LITTLE, BROWN, & CO., BOSTON. THE FOOT-NOTES
AND REFERENCES TO CASES ARE OMITTED.]

THE judicial power of the United States is commensurate with the ordinary legislative and executive powers of the general government, and the powers which concern treaties; but it is also still broader, and in some cases is made to embrace controversies from regard exclusively to the parties suing or sued, irrespective of the nature of the questions in dispute. The cases in which this authority has been given are cases in which the influence of state interests and jealousies upon the administration of state laws might possibly be unfavorable to impartial justice, and which for that reason it was deemed wise to remove to the federal jurisdiction.

Laws for its Exercise.—But although the Constitution extends the power to the cases specified, it does not make complete provision for its exercise, except in the few cases of which the Supreme Court is authorized to take cognizance. For other cases it is necessary that courts shall be created by Congress, and their respective jurisdictions defined; and in creating them Congress may confer upon each so much of the judicial power of the United States as to its wisdom shall seem proper and suitable, and restrict that which is conferred at discretion. In doing so it may apportion among the several federal courts all the judicial power of the United States, or it may apportion a part only, and in that case what is not apportioned will be left to be exercised by the courts of the States. Thus the States may have a limited jurisdiction within the sphere of the judicial power of the United States, but subject to be further limited or wholly taken away by subsequent federal legislation. Such is the state of the law at this time: many cases within the reach of the judicial power of the United States are left wholly to the state courts, while in many others the state courts are permitted to exercise a jurisdiction concurrent with that of the federal courts, but with a final review of their judgments on questions of federal law in the United States Supreme Court.

*　　*　　*　　*　　*　　*　　*　　*　　*

These reasons, however, do not apply to the original jurisdiction over a case, but only to the final application in the case of the rule of law that shall govern it. The full purpose of the federal jurisdiction is subserved if the case, though heard first in the state court, may be removed at the option of the parties for final determination in the courts of the United States. The legislation of Congress has therefore left the parties at liberty, with few exceptions, to bring their suits in the state courts irrespective of the questions involved, but has made provision for protecting the federal authority by a transfer to the federal courts, either before or after judgment, of the cases to which the federal judicial power extends. The exceptions will appear as we proceed.

A case may be said to arise under the Constitution, or under a law or treaty, when a power conferred or supposed to be, a right claimed, a privilege granted, a protection secured, or a prohibition contained therein, is in question. It matters not whether the party immediately concerned be the United States, in its sovereign capacity, asserting one of its most important powers, or a State defending what it believes to be its own reserved jurisdiction, or a humble citizen contending for a trivial interest: if the case turns wholly or in part on the interpretation or application of the Constitution, the validity or construction of an enactment of Congress, the force or extent of a treaty, the justification of any act of a federal officer or agent by the federal authority under which he assumes to act, or the validity of any state enactment, or any act under supposed state authority, which is disputed as an encroachment upon federal jurisdiction, or as being expressly or by implication forbidden by the federal Constitution,—in each instance the case is fairly within the intent of the provision under consideration, and within its reason and necessity.

To give the necessary effect to this provision it has been provided that "a final judgment or decree in any suit in the highest court of a State in which a decision in the suit could be had, where is drawn in question the validity of a treaty or statute of, or an authority exercised under, the United States, and the decision is against their validity ; or where is drawn in question the validity of a statute of, or an authority exercised under, any State, on the ground of their being repugnant to the Constitution, treaties, or laws of the United States, and the decision is in favor of their validity ; or where any title, right, privilege, or immunity is claimed under the Constitution, or any treaty or statute of, or commission held or authority exercised under, the United States, and the decision is against the title, right, privilege, or immunity specially set up or claimed by either party, under such Constitution, treaty, statute, commission, or authority, may be re-examined, and reversed or affirmed in the Supreme Court [of the United States] on a writ of error."

A careful reading of this statute will show that the review in the federal Supreme Court is only provided for, when the decision in the state court is against the title, right, privilege, or immunity set up or claimed under the federal authority. Where the decision does not deny what is thus claimed, the reason for a review is wanting. Nor is it sufficient to authorize the removal of the case to the federal Supreme Court that some one of the enumerated questions might have arisen in or been applicable to it ; it must appear by the record itself, either expressly or by clear and necessary intendment, that some one of them did arise in the state court, and was there passed upon, and the right, title, privilege, or immunity denied.

Cases affecting Ambassadors, etc.—In all cases affecting ambassadors, other public ministers and consuls, and those in which a State shall be a party, the Supreme Court has original jurisdiction. These are the only cases in which original jurisdiction is conferred upon that court, and it cannot be extended by statute. Therefore the court cannot have jurisdiction to issue the writ of mandamus to one of the heads of the executive department, or a writ of certiorari to one of the district judges sitting as commissioner under a treaty, or to a military commission ordered by a general officer of the United States army, commanding a military department which has tried and sentenced a civilian to punishment, or a writ of *habeas corpus*, except as an appellate process. The rule of construction that is applied in these cases is this : that the affirmative words of the Constitution, declaring in what cases the Supreme Court shall have original jurisdiction, must be construed

negatively as to all other cases. Giving the Supreme Court original jurisdiction does not exclude the jurisdiction of other courts,
and therefore cases affecting foreign representatives may originate
in other courts, but they will be subject in such courts to all the
rules of privilege conferred by international law, and to the appellate jurisdiction of the federal Supreme Court. And Congress in
its discretion may, and it has done, exclude altogether the jurisdiction of state tribunals over suits against foreign representatives. As the privileges of ambassadors, ministers, and consuls
are conferred, not for their own advantage, but as the privileges
of their government, it is fit and proper that the courts of the
government to which they are accredited, and with which alone
they can have official dealings, should have exclusive cognizance
of suits against them.

Admiralty and Maritime Cases.—* * * * The federal [ad-
miralty and maritime] jurisdiction will therefore include the case of
collisions on navigable lakes or rivers, of vessels engaged in commerce between ports of the same State, and occurring within the
body of a county, and also the case of contracts of affreightment,
though to be performed within the State where made. So cases of
collision of vessels passing from one navigable body of water to
another, through a connecting canal, like the Welland Canal, are
of federal cognizance. And admiralty has jurisdiction of collisions occurring on tide-water, though the vessel be at a wharf or
pier in the harbor.

The general jurisdiction over the place within a State which is
subject to the grant of admiralty power adheres to the territory,
as a portion of the sovereignty not given away, and the residuary
powers of legislation remain in the States. Therefore the admiralty jurisdiction does not divest the state jurisdiction to punish
crimes. Neither does it divest the state jurisdiction to regulate
the fisheries, and to punish those who trangress the regulations.

Suits by and against the United States.—The United States, like
any other sovereignty, is not suable in its own courts, except with
its own consent; but it may consent, as has been done by creating
and defining the jurisdiction of the Court of Claims. Neither is
the United States suable in a state court, for the United States is
supreme within its sphere, and the States cannot subordinate it to
their authority. It has been quite authoritatively conceded, however, by the federal judiciary, "that land within a State, purchased

by the United States as a mere proprietor, and not reserved or appropriated to any special purpose, may be liable to condemnation for street or highways, like the land of other proprietors, under the rights of eminent domain'"; and the concession will cover all cases of appropriations for public purposes. A right to appropriate implies a right to provide the means whereby a court may obtain jurisdiction, which in these cases may be some other means than the ordinary writs. But the States can have no right to appropriate any portion of the land which has been purchased, or otherwise acquired, by the United States, as a means in the performance of any of its governmental functions ; such as land held for a fortification, or for an arsenal and government manufactory of arms.

As a corporation the United States may sue as plaintiff, in either its own or the state courts, or in the courts of a foreign country, as occasion may require.

Controversies between States.—Many questions might arise under this clause concerning the reach of the federal jurisdiction over controversies between States. the subjects that may be dealt with and determined, and how far the sovereign rights of the States, and the extent of their respective territorial jurisdictions. may be brought within the cognizance and final determination of the federal judiciary. The clause conferring jurisdiction of such controversies is general, and only as cases arise can it be determined whether they present questions which are properly of judicial cognizance as between the States. A question of boundary is plainly such a question, and so is the question whether the conditions in a compact between two States, on the performance of which certain territory was to be detached from the one and become a part of the other, have ever been complied with, so as to effect the transfer.

By "States," in the provision of the Constitution conferring this jurisdiction, is intended the States in the Union. An Indian tribe is neither a State in the Union in this sense, nor a foreign state, and entitled as such to sue in the federal courts.

*   *   *   *   *   *   *   *   *

Suits against States.—The clause of the Constitution which at first conferred the federal jurisdiction extended to suits against States by other States, by citizens of other States, and by foreign states, citizens, or subjects. But by amendment to the Constitution

140   JURISDICTION OF COURTS.

this jurisdiction has been so limited as to be confined to suits
brought by States in the Union, and by foreign states, and the
States are no longer subject to be sued in the federal courts by
private persons. But the fact that a State has an interest in the
controversy, however extensive, will not bring the case under the
amendment and exclude the federal jurisdiction so long as the
State itself is not a party. Therefore a state corporation may be
sued in the federal courts, notwithstanding the State is the sole
stockholder. It is not believed, however, that a State can be
indirectly sued by making its agent or officer the nominal defendant, where the agent or officer merely holds the state property or
securities, or occupies a position of trust under the State, and in
the performance of its duties commits upon others no trespass, so
that the cause of action relied upon must be one in which he would
be responsible only as such agent, officer, or trustee. If such
action were permitted, the eleventh amendment might be nullified.
But where an officer makes himself a trespasser by attempting to
enforce a void authority, it is immaterial to the jurisdiction who
undertook to confer the void authority, since he is responsible individually, on well settled common-law principles.

The force of the eleventh amendment is restricted to original
suits, and it does not preclude a review in the federal Supreme
Court of decisions in the state courts where is drawn in question
any title, right, privilege, or exemption under the Constitution,
laws, or treaties of the United States.

Other Controversies.—Where the jurisdiction of a case depends
upon the citizenship of parties, the fact should appear on inspection of the record. But citizenship in the sense of this provision
means nothing more than residence. A resident in one of the
Territories, or of the District of Columbia, is not entitled to sue
or be sued as a citizen of the State. A corporation created by
and transacting business within a State is for this purpose to be
deemed to represent corporators who are citizens of the State, and
a foreign corporation is to be deemed to represent corporators
who are aliens. As a declaration of intention to become a citizen
under the naturalization laws does not make one a citizen, it will
not preclude an alien suing as such. The courts will not be open
to suits by aliens when their country is at war with our own.

Legislation assigning the Jurisdiction to Courts.—In the exercise of its authority to assign to courts such portion of the judicial

power as it shall determine is proper or needful, Congress has provided by law that the jurisdiction vested in the courts of the United States, in the cases and proceedings following, shall be exclusive of the courts of the several States :—

1. Of all crimes and offences cognizable under the authority of the United States ;

2. Of all suits for penalties and forfeitures incurred under the laws of the United States ;

3. Of all civil causes of admiralty and maritime jurisdiction ; saving to suitors in all cases the right of a common-law remedy where the common law is competent to give it ;

4. Of all seizures under the laws of the United States, on land or waters not within admiralty and maritime jurisdiction ;

5. Of all cases arising under the patent-right or copy-right laws of the United States ;

6. Of all matters and proceedings in bankruptcy ;

7. Of all controversies of a civil nature where a State is a party, except between a State and its citizens, and between a State and citizens of other States or aliens.

Federal courts are also given original jurisdiction of causes of action arising under the postal laws ; suits for drawback of duties ; suits for violations of the statute of the United States for the protection of civil rights, or for the deprivation of rights, privileges, or immunities secured by the Constitution or laws of the United States ; suits to recover the possession of any office,—except legislative offices and the office of Elector of President and Vice-President,—where the sole question touching the title thereto arises out of the denial of the right to vote to any citizen offering to vote, on account of race, color, or previous condition of servitude ; proceedings for the removal from office of any one holding the same contrary to the provisions of the third section of the fourteenth amendment ; and suits by or against the national banks.

Also of suits at common law, where the United States, or any officer thereof, suing under authority of an act of Congress, is plaintiff; suits arising under the revenue laws ; suits arising under any law relative to the slave trade ; and suits brought by any person to recover damages for an injury to person or property on account of any act done by him under any law of the United States for the protection or collection of any of its revenues, or to enforce the rights of citizens of the United States to vote in any State.

Also of suits of a civil nature, at common law or in equity, where the matter in dispute, exclusive of costs, exceeds the sum of five hundred dollars, and an alien is a party, or where the suit is between a citizen of the State where it is brought and a citizen of another State, and suits in equity where the matter in dispute, exclusive of costs, exceeds the sum or value of five hundred dollars, and the United States are petitioners.

Transfer of Causes from State Courts.—As suits may be instituted in the state courts in all cases in which the jurisdiction of the federal courts is not made exclusive, the purpose had in view in conferring the federal power would often be defeated if there were not some provision under which a cause brought in a state court might be removed to a federal court. For example, if a citizen of one State should bring suit in one of its courts against a citizen of another State, the case would be one which by the Constitution is embraced in the grant of the federal power; and the reason why it was included is that it may sometimes happen that local feelings, sentiments, prejudices, or prepossessions may preclude a fair trial in the state court, or at least give rise to fears or suspicions that such may be the case. But it may be and is entirely proper to allow the suit to be thus brought in the first instance, because in most cases no such influences will be suspected or feared, and the parties would go to trial in the state court without objection. But if they are feared, the reasons for referring the case to the federal court are then apparent. A case of more importance to the federal jurisdiction is where a federal officer is sued in a state court, for some act or omission in his office. For many such acts or omissions there is no civil responsibility in any court, but for some there is. The general rule is, that, if a duty imposed upon an officer is exclusively of a public nature, his neglect to perform it can only be punished by some proceeding, either civil or criminal, instituted by the proper public authorities; but if a duty is imposed upon him for the benefit of an individual, the latter has his private action to recover damages for any failure in performance whereby he is injured. The difference between the public and the private duties is well illustrated in cases arising under the post-office laws. The Postmaster-General has duties to perform, which are of high importance to the nation and to all its people; but they are public duties exclusively, and he never becomes charged with obligations to any particular person, so as

---

to be liable to individual actions. It is different with a local postmaster. When mail matter is received at his office, directed to a particular person, it becomes his duty to that person to deliver it on demand, and he is liable to a suit for damages in case of refusal. A like distinction exists between the duties of the Secretary of the Treasury and the collector of the customs at a port: the former is responsible only to the government for the faithful performance of duty; but the latter owes duties to those whose imported goods pass through his hands, and he may become liable to private suits for oppressive conduct and illegal charges. So the duties of the United States marshal, which resemble those of the sheriff, are to a large extent duties to individuals, and may frequently subject him to suits. So any federal officer may become involved in private suits on allegations that, in the pretended discharge of duty, he has trespassed on the rights of third parties. All these, and many others which might be named, are cases coming within the scope of the federal judicial power, and many of them are cases in which it might be exceedingly important to the federal authority that they be referred to the federal courts for final adjudication.

For these cases it is provided by statute that causes may be removed from state to federal courts where the amount in controversy exceeds five hundred dollars, in the following cases:—

1. Where the suit is against an alien, or is by a citizen of the State wherein it is brought and against a citizen of another State, it may be removed on petition of the defendant.

2. Where the suit is against an alien and a citizen of the State wherein it is brought, or is by a citizen of such State against a citizen of the same and a citizen of another State, it may be removed, as against such alien or citizen of another State, on his petition, and the case may proceed in the state court as against the other defendant or defendants.

3. Where the suit is between a citizen of the State in which it is brought and a citizen of another State, it may be removed on petition of the latter, be he plaintiff or defendant, on his filing an affidavit that he has reason to believe, and does believe, that from prejudice or local influence he will not be able to obtain justice in such state court.

* * * * * * * * *

Habeas Corpus.—The Supreme Court and the Circuit and District Courts have power to issue the writ of *habeas corpus*, and the

several justices and judges thereof, within their respective jurisdictions, have also power to issue it, for the purposes of an inquiry into the cause of restraint upon liberty. But in no case
shall the writ extend to a prisoner in jail, unless where he is in
custody under or by color of the authority of the United States;
or is committed for trial before some court thereof; or is in custody for an act done or omitted in pursuance of a law of the
United States, or of an order, process, or decree of a court or
judge thereof; or is in custody in violation of the Constitution, or
of a law or treaty of the United States; or, being a subject or
citizen of a foreign state and domiciled therein, is in custody for
an act done or omitted under any alleged right, title, authority,
privilege, protection, or exemption claimed under the commission
or order or sanction of any foreign state, or under color thereof,
the validity and effect whereof depend upon the law of nations; or
unless it is necessary to bring the prisoner into court to testify.
This last is a provision for facilitating the investigation of facts
in federal tribunals, and all the other cases mentioned are cases in
which the national authority is in some way involved. The
Federal Supreme Court also has authority to issue the writ in the
exercise of its appellate jurisdiction.

The general authority to examine, by means of this writ, into
unlawful restraints upon personal liberty, has not been conferred
upon the United States, and therefore remains with the States.
But if state tribunals issue the writ for a prisoner detained under
federal authority, it must be dismissed when return is made showing the facts. A prisoner held under state process for extradition
to another State may have a *habeas corpus* from a federal court or
judge; the process of extradition being provided for by, and taken
under, the Constitution of the United States.

Conflict of Jurisdiction.—In strictness there can be no such
thing as a conflict of laws between State and nation. The laws of
both operate within the same territory, but if in any particular
case their provisions are in conflict, one or the other is void. If a
law of Congress is passed upon a subject which is within its constitutional powers, any state legislation opposed to it is a mere
nullity. For this reason state statutes which in their operation
would impede the execution of the Fugitive Slave Law were mere
futile attempts to make laws, and were to be held void by the state
judiciary as well as by the federal. So are all state laws which

tend to impede or obstruct the laws passed by Congress under its power to regulate commerce, all which undertake to levy taxes on the means selected by the general government for use in the exercise of its essential powers, and so on. On the other hand, a federal enactment taxing a State or its municipal corporations is inoperative, and so is one undertaking to establish regulations of local commerce within the States, and it cannot interfere with the operation of state laws on the same subject. In these cases the federal and state courts, if the question came before them, would recognize the same rule, and each administer the same law. If they chanced to differ in opinion, an appeal to the Federal Supreme Court must determine the controversy.

But questions of much delicacy sometimes arise, when the federal and state courts, under their concurrent authority, may find their respective jurisdictions invoked in the same controversy. This might lead to collisions, and to unseemly and perhaps dangerous controversies, if the action of the courts were not directed by certain rules of good sense and comity devised to preserve harmony and insure an orderly administration of justice.

The most important of these rules is that the court which first obtains jurisdiction of a controversy by the service of process, will not be interfered with by the other in the exercise of that jurisdiction until final judgment and execution. The federal courts will not therefore enjoin the proceedings in a suit in a state court, nor a state court those in a federal court.

Political Questions.—Over political questions the courts have no authority, but must accept the determination of the political departments of the government as conclusive. Such are the questions of the existence of war, the restoration of peace, the *de facto* or rightful government of another country, the authority of foreign ambassadors and ministers, the admission of a State to the Union, the restoration to constitutional relations of a State lately in rebellion, the extent of the jurisdiction of a foreign power, the right of Indians to recognition as a tribe, and so on.

Final Authority in Construction.—The several departments of the government are equal in dignity and of co-ordinate authority, and neither can subject the other to its jurisdiction, or strip it of any portion of its constitutional powers. But the judiciary is the final authority in the construction of the constitution and the laws, and its construction should be received and followed by the other departments. This results from the nature of its jurisdiction; questions of construction arise in legal controversies, and are determined by the courts, and when determined the courts have power to give effect to their conclusions. Their judgments thus become the law of the land on the points covered by them, and a disregard of them, whether by private citizens or by officers of the government, could only result in new controversy, to be finally determined by the judiciary in the same way. But the courts have no authority to pass upon abstract questions, or questions not presented by actual litigation, and have therefore nothing to do with questions which relate exclusively to executive or legislative authority; nor is there any method in which their opinions can be constitutionally expressed, so as to have binding force upon either the executive or the legislature when the question presents itself, not as one of existing law, but as one of what it is proper or politic or competent to make law for the future. The judiciary, though the final judge of what the law is, is not the judge of what the law should be.

It is very proper, however, that the judiciary, in passing upon questions of law which have been considered and acted upon by the other departments, should give great weight to their opinions, especially if they have passed unchallenged for a considerable period. The judiciary have often yielded to it when the correctness of a practical construction of the law by the executive departments, in the performance of their own duties, was in question; but they cannot do this when, in the opinion of the court, the construction is plainly in violation of the Constitution.

CONTENTS:

www.ingramcontent.com/pod-product-compliance
Lightning Source LLC
Chambersburg PA
CBHW020559270326
41927CB00006B/897